THE DAY
THE CHURCH DIED

KEVIN MILLS

The Day the Church Died

© 2024 Kevin Mills
© 2024 Church Answers

All rights reserved.

ISBN 979-8-9883649-4-8

Church Answers
Franklin, TN

Printed in the United States of America

CONTENTS

Consider how far you have fallen! Repent and do the things you did at first. If you do not repent, I will come to you and remove your lampstand from its place.
Revelation 2:5

Prologue

I f you've ever invested in a mutual fund, you have undoubtedly received a prospectus containing detailed information about the fund's investments. These documents will always include data concerning the historical annual gains and losses of the fund. Within every prospectus will be a disclaimer referencing the risks involved with investing monies in the fund. Within the disclaimer will be a sentence that reads like the following: *Past performance does not guarantee future results.* In other words, just because the fund had positive gains in the past does not necessarily ensure future success. However, the past performance is included because it indicates what will *most likely* be the future growth or decline of the fund.

A 2024 prospectus on the American church would show historical losses, year after year, for at least the last two decades. You can picture this line on a graph going from the top left to the bottom right section of the page.

This book extends that graph.

In your hands is a fictional account of a research project completed in 2071. As of this writing, that is less than fifty years into the future. I most likely will not be alive to see the state of our nation and the American church, but my children probably will.

Their generation will get to experience either a renewal of the church or her decline and eventual death. Only the Lord knows which will be reality.

Over the last several years, much has been written about the state of Christianity in the United States. According to Gallup, less than half of United States residents are members of any church, synagogue, or mosque.[1] In the last twenty years, the average attendance at a church worship service has been cut in half, from 137 attendees to 65.[2] Recently, Jim Davis and Michael Graham released the astonishing results of their extensive surveys and research in a work entitled *The Great Dechurching*. This book details the extensive movement of Americans away from the church. Over the last several decades, forty million former churchgoers in our nation have quit attending. It is the most significant religious shift in the history of our nation.[3]

I could bore you with dozens of other recent surveys and articles bemoaning the deteriorating state of the American church. Just ten years ago, I would have taken the time to do precisely that. However, I know of few churchgoers (and perhaps non-churchgoers) who believe the church in America is thriving. Even the most casual observer can see the feebleness of the body of Christ in this nation.

This book is not an attempt to analyze the current situation. Instead, based on trends, articles, news reports, conversations with other pastors, and simply observing the changes in our culture, this is a (perhaps) fictional account of how the story of the church in America ends.

Please understand: I am an optimist by nature. I have spent my entire adult life serving the body of Christ. I believe the church is the hope of the world.

As well, I'm working, praying, and hoping against the words written on the pages of this book. I vehemently believe in a God who touches hearts, forgives sinners, redeems brokenness, heals hurts, and changes the mindsets of individuals. I would love nothing more than to wake up one morning and read a headline proclaiming the *Next Great Awakening* had descended upon America. I firmly believe this *could* happen. It would be wonderful to see the Spirit of God sweep across this nation and completely change our culture.

But, I also want to recognize the reality of what is happening around us. Even with hard evidence staring us in the face, I hear very few pastors and other church leaders sounding the alarm. Those who do so find their warnings falling on deaf ears. Most Christians haven't stopped to consider the inevitable conclusion to the story of the church in America.

This book attempts to paint the picture of our nation's future if the church in America continues in the same direction. Some will say I'm being extreme. They will claim that I'm exaggerating and being overly dramatic. Or that I'm the proverbial chicken who gets hit in the head by an acorn, and then runs around screaming that the sky is falling. I understand these sentiments. Some of the pictures I paint of America thirty and forty years from now seem improbable to most of us living in the 2020s.

Imagine, however, a book written forty years ago about life in our nation today—a fictional account of a 2024 America. The author describes, let's say, a group of people seated at a table in a restaurant. Instead of hearing scattered conversations between these patrons, there is complete silence. The diners sit in their chairs with their heads down, all completely engrossed in hand-held electronic devices. The author explains that one lady at the table uses her fingers to type a message to her son, who lives in Russia (not the Soviet Union, but *Russia*). This message is immediately read by her son, and Mom just as instantaneously reads his reply. Moreover, few words are typed. This lady chuckles at the "emojis," "memes," and "gifs" appearing on her electronic device, all sent by her son who is *thousands of miles away*, yet able to communicate with his mom in a non-verbal yet real-time "conversation."

Can you hear the comments from those living in America forty years ago? Readers would have scoffed and said, "This is nothing but science fiction. This is a modern version of George Orwell's *1984*, written almost forty years ago about a dystopian world that never became reality. The same will be true with this book."

Of course, those nay-sayers would have been entirely wrong.

Or imagine the author describing a high school track meet where biological males can participate in girls' competitive events. These boys claim that while they were assigned the male gender at birth, in reality, they are females. The author includes an account of a sports star criticizing these schools for allowing males to compete against females. While this famous athlete is a former hero of the LGBTQ+ movement, her comments are quickly condemned. She is labeled a "transphobic," and she is subsequently dropped as a spokesperson for a sports non-profit organization.

Most readers would've laughed and said, "How ridiculous. Boys competing in girls' sporting events? Never. You might as well have written a story about Olympic gold medal winner Bruce Jenner becoming a girl. Absolutely absurd!"

Assume this author told the story of a parent telling her friends and neighbors that her 4-year-old son was really a girl simply because he liked to play with dolls instead of trucks. Imagine a scene in which an American beer manufacturer celebrated a biological male's "transition" to female. Or the author writing about physicians prescribing puberty-blocking medications for children—not because of an acute medical need—but simply because a child believed their biological gender didn't match with their inner self.

"No doctor in the world would do something like that," readers would've said. "The first rule in medical ethics is 'do no harm.' Puberty-blockers would certainly lead to long-term, harmful effects."

Suppose the author included language about those in the highest levels of our government using terms like "birthing-person" and "non-birthing person" to describe men and women. Or a nation where it was not only legal for same-sex partners to marry, but major Christian denominations fully endorsed these unions. Or high school students identifying as "furries" and demanding their principals put litter boxes in the school restrooms to accommodate their bathroom needs. Or public libraries routinely allowing drag queens to read books to children but refusing a Christian actor an opportunity to read his book.

"Nonsense," they would have exclaimed. "Kids claiming to be cats? Drag queens reading to our children? Never going to happen."

Or a society in which there existed unfettered access to free pornographic material for every person with an electronic device and an internet connection. Or that these websites would be among the nation's most visited. Or that millions of people would take photos and videos of themselves engaging in various sexual activities and upload those to these sites.

"Pure fantasy," they would have said. "You're just trying to scare people. You're being way too far-fetched. Our culture could never become that depraved."

Or that our national debt would exceed thirty *trillion* dollars. Or that state and local governments would issue mandates against church members gathering for worship. Or that a federal agency would target Catholics as potential terrorists. Or that suicide would become one of the leading causes of death among young adults. Or that kids would walk into their high school and shoot their fellow students and teachers before turning those same guns on themselves.

"Impossible. Sounds like the *Mad Max* movie to me. There is no way that will ever be the condition of our nation."

Again, time would have proven them wrong. The above paragraphs describe the reality of our modern culture. This work of fiction has become life in America today.

This book picks up where that not-so-imaginary novel ends. As mentioned above, this is an attempt to extend the graph. If we continue in the same direction, what will be the state of the American church and the American culture? The following pages are my effort to answer that question.

Additionally, this book is written from the perspective of a researcher who is very much the product of a post-Christian America. This fictional author approaches this project with a thoroughly secular worldview and—throughout the book—expresses opinions and offers conclusions emerging from this frame of reference. There are times this imaginary writer is mistaken about Christian beliefs. Moreover, the author's value system is thoroughly secular. While attempting to be an "objective" researcher, the anti-Christian biases of the researcher are quite apparent.

I trust you realize that these are, obviously, not my personal opinions or beliefs. Rather, I believe this is the most effective approach to paint a picture of the church in America—and America herself—decades from now. That is, assuming the church and American culture continue in the same direction.

I have also been careful to connect the dots for you, the reader. The following chapters contain actual past quotes, events, and statistics intertwined with fictional future quotes, events, and statistics. The purpose of this is to show you, the reader, the next chapters in the life of the American church and American culture. This is, as stated above, my attempt to extend the graph of where both are potentially headed.

There are times, admittedly, when this will possibly cause confusion. You, the reader, will wonder whether a quote is fact or fiction. Here is how you can know the difference between the two: the events, quotes, statistics, etc., occurring before January 1, 2024, are actual and footnoted.

Those dated January 1, 2024, or later are simply speculation and solely the creation of this author's imagination.

None of them have actually happened.

Yet.

Kevin Mills
January 2024

September 15, 2071

The church died on June 12, 2061.

Finding an exact day and time to mark the death of the church in America was no easy task. Other researchers have and will quibble with my pronouncement. Some will argue that the body of Christ was dead years before this particular date. A few will point to evidence of a faint heartbeat existing in the years after 2061. I understand the reasons for each side of this debate. However, this date is not arbitrary. I chose June 12, 2061, for a specific reason.

That was the date City Church in Phoenix, Arizona closed its doors. A final service was held on that beautiful summer Sunday morning. For over three decades, this campus welcomed thousands of individuals gathering to worship. The auditorium hosted multiple services each weekend to accommodate the crowd of attendees. Yet, on June 12, 2061, only twenty-two individuals were present for this last meeting.

After years of decline in membership and constant friction with county and state governments, the church decided to sell its property and buildings to the electric car manufacturer *Endura*. According to church and county officials, the sales price matched, almost exactly, the total amount owed by the church in taxes due to the county government and to various creditors, suppliers, and utility companies. For nearly a decade before closing, the church attempted various measures to maintain financial solvency, including selling portions of its extremely valuable land. However, another decline in donations, exacerbated by the laws enacted in the state of Arizona to limit amounts given to Christian churches, caused the church to come to the fateful decision to finally dissolve the organization.

Exactly twenty-two members—mostly octogenarians—gathered in City Church's worship center. Completed in 2031, the room originally held 3,500 individuals. In its heyday, the church held four Sunday morning worship services and one Saturday evening service to accommodate the more than 12,000 individuals who gathered on the church campus each weekend. However, the church experienced a dramatic decline in the 2040s. Eventually, the worship space became far too cavernous for the approximately 1,500 still faithfully attending each week. City Church raised the funds to remodel and downsize their worship center. The new space only held 1,300 and allowed the church to return to multiple worship gatherings each Sunday, but in a much smaller venue.

Over time, though, the church continued to decline in membership and regular worship attendance. Throughout the late 2040s and early 2050s, church leaders constantly adjusted to a new normal. Eventually, they returned to one Sunday morning worship service. A few years later, the church pastors installed heavy black curtains in the rear third of the worship center to reduce the size of the space, trying to better accommodate the dwindling numbers who gathered.

Eventually, by 2055, the writing was on the wall. The end of the church was inevitable. The few dozen remaining individuals tried to reimagine, redesign, relaunch, and regroup, but no amount of *re's* could revive this dying church. Finally, in the summer of 2059, congregational representatives met with an attorney, a commercial real estate agent, and two county officials. City Church was allowed to quietly dissolve when *Endura* offered to purchase the property. Only the top executives knew that this church campus would soon transition into a sales center for their new self-driving electric vehicles.

In January of 2061, the deal finally closed. The contract allowed the few remaining members to continue meeting on the campus until the end of the year. However, after pressure from its employees and threats of a boycott on social media over perceived support of the church, *Endura* decided to break the terms of the contract. The letter from the company's chief legal counsel notified City Church that June 12, 2061, was the last day they were permitted to meet on *Endura's* campus. The remainder of the letter stated, in essence: *Sue us if you dare.*

These new owners of the church property allowed this final worship gathering only as a memorial to the past. They gave clear, strict guidelines about the content and length of this service. No Bible passages were to be read. Permission was granted for one prayer as long as the person offering the prayer didn't mention the name of Jesus. References to past events were allowed only if they weren't overly religious in their content.

An article posted on the website *Metro Life* described this final gathering of City Church. The memorial service opened with what could only be described as a general prayer generally

11

prayed to a general god who generally did not care about the events of the morning. After the lackluster prayer and the concluding "Amen," the attendees watched a fifteen-minute video of past pictures and footage of City Church. The founding pastor, Joey Donavan, was prominently featured. Snippets of his sermons played, although only parts considered non-religious: portions from messages on dealing with worry, finding financial freedom, and parenting teenagers. The video also showed Mr. Donavan interviewing the 2032 Democratic and Republican nominees for President of the United States.

There were pictures of large crowds gathering in the original and the later resized worship centers. The video contained footage of church members working at an orphanage in Haiti, digging a well in Africa, and handing out food and clothing at a homeless shelter in Phoenix.

The video tribute ended with comments by James Hatcher, a former City Church pastor who now leads a church in Uganda. He smiled as he talked about the church hiring him in 2049 when he was only 28 years old. He thanked them for following his leadership, even as the church faced dramatically declining attendance numbers each year. He spoke briefly about his decision to move to Uganda, where churches were growing exponentially. Finally, he talked about the legacy of City Church, not so much in the United States but in other places around the world.

At the conclusion of the video, Daniel Wood, the youngest member of the church, made his way to the podium. He described his journey to City Church, which happened just after the COVID pandemic of 2020. He was in first grade. A school friend approached him one day and asked, "Do you believe in God?"

Religion wasn't a part of his home, he said, and so his response was, "What's a god?" This classmate invited him to a children's event at his church that Friday night. "And there," said Mr. Wood, "my life was forever changed. I'm not allowed to talk about how it was changed, but those of you from the church who are gathered here know why it did." He then thanked everyone, not so much for being present that morning, but for the years they dedicated themselves to the church. Mr. Wood then returned to his seat.

Quickly, another gentleman walked to the podium and introduced himself as Allen McCauley, the public relations director for *Endura*. He thanked those in attendance for coming and informed them that this now concluded the memorial service for City Church. He invited them to gather in the courtyard for refreshments and reminded them to stop by the brand-new vehicle showroom before leaving.

The *Metro Life* reporter, Jamal Allen, ended his piece with the following account of what he witnessed on this fateful day:

> I watched the individuals slowly collect their belongings and head outside. I joined the small crowd, curious about their conversations. What would they say about City Church's post-mortem state? Did anyone really care? What would they do next?
>
> I noticed one gentleman seated on a bench, balancing a small plate of hors d'oeuvres on his lap. I walked over and asked if I could sit next to him. He shrugged his shoulders and pointed to the empty seat to his right, indicating his willingness to share the bench. We sat silently for a few moments, enjoying the warm Arizona sunshine. After a

couple of minutes, I turned to him and said, "So, what did you think about the memorial service?"

His gaze shifted from his plate to the people milling around in the courtyard. For several seconds, he did not speak. I silently wondered if he'd heard my question. But, finally, he took a deep breath and slowly said, "You know, all morning long, this one phrase has been continually running through my mind."

He paused again, long enough that I thought he might not actually share this phrase with me. Eventually, he turned his head and looked directly at me. His eyes were wet with tears. "You want to know it?" he asked.

"Absolutely."

He turned and looked back out at the courtyard. "These four words keep rolling around in my brain: *What could have been.*"

The article appeared on *Metro Life's* website, buried at the bottom corner of the page for one day, and relegated the next to a subcategory labeled *Around Town*. It received fewer than 500 hits. No one really cared. The news could've just as easily been about the closing of the last combustible engine factory. Interesting to historians, perhaps, but with zero impact on the daily lives of most Americans.

A Major Shift in Perspective

In my opinion, that was the day the church in America died. I chose the final meeting of City Church as the time of death for two reasons.

First, City Church had been a very large congregation, considered a mega church for much of its history. The church began in 2025 and—as the population of Phoenix exploded in growth—so did the church membership. By 2030, the church hosted thousands of individuals meeting in several different rented spaces located throughout the suburbs of Phoenix. After the construction of its new worship center in 2031, City Church grew even more rapidly, eventually seeing attendance approach 15,000 on many weekends during its heyday. The decline and eventual death of a church the size of City Church represented a watershed moment in Christian America.

Second, and more importantly, the church and its founding pastor, Joey Donavan, were at one time well-known and well-liked among the general population. Donavan's book, *The God Connection*, sold over 50 million copies and in 2030, became part of the national conversation after the suicide attempt by Thomas Ellis in New York City. Ellis was a former hedge fund manager and author of a popular investment strategy website. After the stock market crash that October, Ellis climbed atop the ledge of his 60-story penthouse apartment, intending to leap to his death. A resident of the building across the street saw Ellis and called 911. Emergency personnel (and news reporters) quickly gathered on the street below, frantically crafting a plan to prevent this potential fatality.

However, it was Ellis' girlfriend, Amanda Kelsey, who became the hero of the moment. She had recently purchased and read Pastor Donavan's book. She walked out onto the balcony and calmly but desperately pleaded with Ellis to reconsider his decision. He firmly refused and told her to go back inside, threatening to jump if she came any closer. The following is Kelsey's account of what followed:

> I told him, "I have a book with me, and I'd like to read just a portion to you before you jump." I read from page 133, which talked about the God-shaped hole in all our hearts; a hole that can only be filled by a relationship with God. I told him that I had been trying to fill that hole with lots of things that just wouldn't work. And that I had recently made the decision to see if a relationship with God could do it; to fill this void in my life. And that I thought he needed to do the same. He stared at me hard, like he was looking right through me. Then he said, "Read that part to me again." So, I did. And he said, "You really think God cares anything at all about me?" I told him I did. He stood there for a long time, but then stepped down from the ledge and said, "Okay, let's talk."

In the numerous interviews following this traumatic ordeal, Kelsey highlighted the impact Donavan's book had on her boyfriend and the fact that she believed the words she read saved his life. Both Donavan and *The God Connection* received high praise from multiple media outlets. The fact that such favorable opinions were expressed regarding this dogmatically religious book seems unthinkable to our modern minds. This account demonstrates the level of support for religion in general and Joey Donavan in particular during this period in our nation's history.

In 2032, Donavan's standing in the public eye was so influential that the two major political party candidates for President accepted his invitation to be interviewed on the campus of City Church, in their newly constructed worship center, and in front of a crowd comprised mostly of City Church members. Unbelievably, Mr. Donavan interviewed these two individuals seeking our nation's highest office, and there were no significant objections. There was zero public outcry. Everyone knew one of these individuals would become the next President of the United States. Yet, somehow, it was perfectly acceptable for a Christian pastor to interview them in his church and in front of an audience comprised mostly of Christians. Moreover, the event was broadcast on multiple national news networks, exposing millions of Americans to Mr. Donavan's questions and viewpoints.

These facts all denote just how much our culture had a generally positive view of this church and its pastor. Prior to his retirement from City Church, Donavan would have been considered by many to be "America's Pastor." An article written immediately following the Donavan interview of the two Presidential candidates stated the following:

> First it was Billy Graham. He preached to millions and was welcomed with open arms, across this nation, in every city where he held revivals. Nearly all Americans had a favorable opinion of Dr. Graham and looked to him for spiritual guidance.

After Dr. Graham, it unquestionably became Joey Donavan. His easy-to-understand manner of communicating practical truths resonates with his listeners. Donavan's sermons are widely shared across the internet. Snippets of these messages are shared, liked, and shared again across multiple social media platforms. His book garnered tremendous media attention in the aftermath of the Thomas Ellis affair. And now, Pastor Donavan has become a household name after the recent town hall interviews with both candidates for President. Whether he has sought the position or not is unknown. What is certainly clear is that Donavan is *the* individual most trusted for spiritual guidance among Americans today.

For the first decade of its existence, most Americans viewed both City Church and its pastor quite favorably. The significance of this church moving to *persona-non-grata* status and eventually dissolving cannot be overstated. There was a dramatic sea change in public perception of Christians and the Christian church in the 21st century. The life and death of City Church are a perfect picture of this transformation.

While one could argue that the closing of one former megachurch doesn't accurately mark the time of death of the church in America, the reality of its demise isn't in question. Today, the church is nothing more than a relic of the past. It is as outdated as coal-powered electricity. Sure, the existence of both was vital in building this nation; however, they are wholly unnecessary in our modern culture.

While a few churches still exist, almost none meet on the campuses they owned and operated twenty and thirty years ago.

Across this country, worship centers and buildings with classrooms have been repurposed. Many are now restaurants, bars, condo complexes, office spaces, and funeral homes.

In many cases, the property was sold to a developer who completely razed the buildings. The site of First Baptist Church of Mapleton—once a well-known megachurch in Georgia—is today *Wildwaves Water Park*. While this amusement park welcomes thousands of visitors each year, there is no evidence of the church that formerly occupied the land.

Ascension Church in Jacksonville, Florida began meeting in the early 2020s. The rapid population growth of Florida throughout the 2020s and 2030s contributed greatly to the expansion of the church. Within a decade of opening its doors, Ascension Church had multiple campuses and welcomed several thousand meeting in worship services throughout the week. In 2058, however, the church completely dissolved. Today, their main campus is the home of Sharon Pharmaceuticals, where the cancer-killing drug *Xcaolor* is manufactured.

Lakeside Church in Tulsa, Oklahoma, was the largest church in the state throughout the 2030s. Today, their former campus houses the Johnson Center for Performing Arts. In 2052, the church moved to a leased space in an office complex on the north side of Tulsa. The property owners informed the church leaders that, as part of the lease agreement, they wouldn't be allowed to possess or read the Bible in their meetings. These leaders agreed. Their gatherings today would be considered by most to be a large support group rather than a church.

For decades, Christ Methodist Church in Birmingham, Alabama, hosted thousands of worshippers each weekend for

Sunday services, and during the week, a private school with over 2,000 students used their campus for education and activities. Today, Shelby County School of the Arts occupies the property where the church and Christian school once operated.

Earlier this century, Dogwood Baptist Church in Saint Louis, Missouri, welcomed thousands to their campus for worship on Sundays and throughout the week at their various sporting activities. Today, their campus is the site of *The Vistas*, an upscale apartment complex where residents pay anywhere from $30,000-$40,000 per month for a one- or two-bedroom apartment.

There are countless other accounts of churches dying and their campuses being repurposed. Many of their stories will be told in this book.

From Majority to Minority Status

The church universal has historically thrived under persecution. The earliest Christians faced an extremely hostile Roman government as well as abuse and discrimination from society at large. Yet, the church grew at an exponential rate. Hundreds of thousands of Roman citizens embraced the message of Christ. When Emperor Constantine converted in AD 312, Christianity had already become the dominant religion of the Roman Empire. The oppressive policies of Constantine's predecessors toward Christianity only strengthened the early church.

A contemporary example of this phenomenon is China's transition from communism to a democracy and majority Christian nation. For over one hundred years, the Communist Chinese government took a hardline stance against the Christian church. Pastors were often imprisoned for hosting worship services in their homes. Bibles were confiscated. Christians weren't allowed to hold government jobs or positions of leadership within Chinese corporations.

Yet, this oppression ignited the growth of the church. In 2041, it was estimated that nearly one-third of Chinese citizens were professing Christians. The groundswell of the church continued even under the extreme and widespread persecution of the communist government.

Modern-day China began in 2044 when President Jiang converted to Christianity. The world watched as—seemingly overnight—countless members of the communist party either declared their already secret allegiance to Christ or their desire to become Christians. Over the next two years, the Chinese government adopted a constitution similar to the one ratified by the United States in 1788, although this version contains references not only to God but also to Jesus.

Today, China is known as a place for freedom, democracy, and opportunity. Moreover, the Christian church in China has, for the last twenty-five years, sent countless missionaries throughout the world. The influx of Chinese Christians into the United States eventually led Congress, in 2065, to pass the *Border Protection Act*, which, in part, terminated all visas for Chinese citizens. Within weeks after the passage of this law, thousands of Chinese citizens were physically forced to leave their homes in the United States, and no future visas were granted.

Like the Roman Empire, the church's explosion under persecution led to the eventual embracing of Christianity by the Chinese people and government.

However, the Christian church did not thrive under persecution in the United States. The American church simply could not make the transition from representing a majority of the population to a minority status. Moreover, the church could not shift from existing in a culture favorable toward Christianity to withstanding the restrictions imposed upon it.

The transition seemed slow and incremental to those who lived through the changes. The "frog in the kettle" illustration could be appropriately applied in this situation.

Yet, from a historical viewpoint, the changes were swift. One could argue that the first cultural turn against Christianity occurred on June 25, 1962, less than one hundred years before the death of the church. That was the day the United States Supreme Court declared prayer in public schools unconstitutional.[4] Although this was the first step toward removing Christian influence in the public square, Christianity retained its favored status in the eyes of most Americans. For decades, the culture considered church attendance and membership to be positive in nature. Presidents and other politicians, both Democrats and Republicans, wanted to be seen leaving a church worship service with their Bible in hand. Many members of Congress attended the annual Congressional Prayer Breakfast. Most policies supported Christians and their beliefs.

A perfect example of this past favored status is seen in how President Bill Clinton, a Democrat, signed into law the Defense of Marriage Act (DOMA) on September 21, 1996.[5] In 2008, then-candidate Barack Obama claimed to support "traditional marriage" in his run for President,[6] a view embraced by most Christians.

A few short years later, however, the United States Supreme Court ruled DOMA's laws unconstitutional in cases such as *United States v. Windsor* (2013) and *Obergefell v. Hodges* (2015).[7] After 2012, virtually every Democratic candidate for major offices expressed their support for same-sex marriage, a dramatic shift from the words and actions of Democratic Presidents Clinton and Obama.

For the first time in its history, the church in America faced a culture that defined the institution of marriage in radically different ways from both historical and Christian traditions. It was a defining moment for the church. Christian leaders were forced to wrestle with numerous questions. *How do we respond to accusations of discrimination and bigotry regarding our view on marriage? Why do we believe in a traditional view of marriage? Is this a nonnegotiable belief, or should we allow different opinions on marriage among Christians?*

This is just one example of how the church in America suddenly found itself swimming against the current of popular culture. From 2020 forward, the friction between the church and society continued to intensify, causing Christians to increasingly move out of favor with the culture. In the 2030s, 40s, and 50s, the severely weakened Christian church in America couldn't endure the growing persecution.

The purpose of this book is to identify the reasons behind its death. Included are several case studies pieced together through various archived blogs. In my research, I identified twelve primary causes behind the decline and demise of the American church. All were contributing factors. All were interconnected. Do not think of these as individual slices of a pie. One is unable to lift out a single factor independently of the others. Instead, they are threads woven together to form the death shroud of the church.

None alone could've destroyed it.

Combined, however, the survival of the church was impossible.

Following are the twelve reasons the church in America died.

CHAPTER 1

A BAD CASE OF MYOPATHY

Preferences and Individualism in the Church

Throughout its history, there have been times of conflict between both individuals and various factions within the Christian church. Although current law doesn't allow me to use the Bible as a primary source, I found several archived blog articles citing disagreements within the early church referenced in the Christian scriptures. While the modern reader certainly recognizes the Bible's lack of reliability as a primary source, the conflicts reportedly described in its pages seem to fit with other historical documents regarding disagreements within the worldwide church. Over the centuries, disputes have been an ever-present reality among Christians. The most notable division was the Protestant Reformation in Europe during the 1500s, a quarrel that led to the formation of many different denominations within Christianity.

Historically, these disagreements between church members and leaders mostly centered around differing beliefs. The Protestant Reformation mentioned above is a prime example. A monk named Martin Luther challenged the Catholic Church's beliefs and the Pope's authority. He and other Christians ultimately broke away from the Catholic Church and formed separate denominations. These sharp divisions came from the inability to agree on numerous theological doctrines.

Sometime around 1980, though, the fights within the American church took on a decidedly different tone. Rather than fighting over *beliefs*, church members and leaders fought over *preferences*. Individual Christians wanted a particular style of music, their favorite type of program, a certain kind of pastor, or a specific color of carpet in the church worship center. Members fought vigorously over these issues. Salvation, the nature of Jesus, and the authority of the Bible rarely divided individual churches. The fights and separations happened over more pedestrian matters.

This particularly divisive period of the American church seems to be unique in the story of Christianity. No historical documents allude to disagreements within churches over *preferences* anywhere close to the scale of what happened in the American church toward the end of the 20th century. Individual opinions and wants took priority over the mission of the church. Countless articles and blogs referenced churches essentially imploding over non-theological, non-mission-critical issues. These churches took on a distinctly myopic posture. Instead of a battleship called to a specific assignment, they viewed their churches as cruise ships there to satisfy their desires.

The Organ Or Drums?

The most common division within these churches centered around musical preferences. In the mid to late 1980s, a new style of musical worship was introduced into many American churches. Before this period, the organ and piano were the primary instruments used to accompany singing. The only significant exception was in a brand of churches known as "Charismatic." These Christians used drums and guitars in their gatherings years before this style of worship became popular among other Protestant denominations.

However, in the late 1980s—and more extensively in the 1990s—many churches introduced this more modern style of music into their corporate gatherings. The primary reason for this change was an attempt to appeal to a younger generation of Christians who viewed church in general and worship specifically as "old-fashioned." The inclusion of these modern musical instruments, it was believed, would provide a way for younger individuals to engage in worship gatherings.

Except, in many cases, these changes brought strong objections from a portion of the church congregation. Numerous archived blogs and articles referred to these disagreements as "Worship Wars." The introduction of this modern style led to intense battles. Those who preferred the old hymns grumbled about this new, contemporary style of worship. Those who enjoyed the modern praise choruses belittled the tired, old-fashioned hymns. Often, these internal divisions became the church's primary focus, causing members to lose sight of any external outreach or missions efforts.

On an archived website entitled *The Theology of Work*, author Mark Roberts wrote:

> When I first became the pastor of Irvine Presbyterian Church, I heard loud and clear from the traditional folk that I must not abandon the traditional hymns and strong

choral music program of the church. Yet, dozens of members begged me to banish "those tired, old hymns that
nobody can sing" in favor of guitar-led praise songs. Hymns
vs. songs, choir vs. band ... it was a classic worship war.[8]

Many other congregations also fought bitterly over the style of
music played in their worship gatherings. Some members wanted
the modern format because it was what they preferred. Others
wanted the traditional songs because that was their musical pref-
erence. Heels dug in hard, and many of the battles were bloody.
Worship pastors were fired. Senior pastors were dismissed. I discovered numerous accounts of churches voting to terminate their
pastor, followed by the pastor leaving and immediately forming
another church in the community. In the process, some members
became disillusioned with the church and quit going altogether.
Others left the former congregation and joined the new church
formed by the terminated pastor. Individuals in the community
heard about the church fight, giving them yet another reason to
dismiss church altogether. The old church that fired the pastor
and the new church started by the dismissed pastor would both
struggle financially and in finding volunteers for their various
programs. Neither would manage to engage or influence the community. In many cases, one or both churches would dissolve and
see their members scatter.

The major worship wars largely ended around 2010. By this
time, most Christian churches had settled on their preferred style
of music. The battles were over; however, in the aftermath, many
congregations were left wounded and weakened.

WHAT HAVE YOU DONE FOR ME LATELY?

Although music was the primary focus of these divisions, it was simply an outward expression of an inner reality. Members viewed their churches as a place where they would be served rather than a place where they would serve others. Most church leaders found it difficult to get members to volunteer, especially in the preschool, children's, and student ministries. Physical changes to a campus often resulted in long business meetings with heated discussions. Numerous blogs referenced "sacred cows" in churches, a term used to identify programs or physical elements of the campus considered to be untouchable or unchangeable. One blog mentioned a two-hour business meeting to discuss removing an old oak tree from the campus of the church. Although the roots caused significant damage to the asphalt parking lot, certain members had a sentimental attachment to this tree that "had always been there as long as we've been attending this church." The congregation voted to remove the tree, and three families became so angry they left the church.

Certain church traditions were also sacred in the minds of members. Recognizing members and including specific songs in worship gatherings were of the highest importance. Individuals fought vigorously for these traditions, but not because they believed them to be essential for the church fulfilling its purpose. Rather, these were personal preferences. Many members took a consumer posture in their relationship with the church. They viewed themselves as customers in a store, clients of a business, or guests at a resort. They came to church services and programs expecting to be served by others.

Additionally, few members gave financially to their churches. Several studies showed that less than half of members gave any amount at all, and only 30 percent gave over $1000 annually. Even in the early 2000s, when the cost of living was far less than today, $1000 in a single year wasn't considered to be a significant sum of money for the average American. Simply put, most churchgoers weren't willing to make personal sacrifices for the sake of their church.

This myopic approach by members greatly undermined the ministries of churches throughout the United States. This inward focus severely weakened numerous congregations to the point that, when the external persecutions came in the 20s and 30s, the church in America wasn't strong enough to survive. This thread served as a crucial component of the garment that ultimately led to the death of the church.

The Rise and Fall of First Church

A website from the 2040s devoted exclusively to accounts of church closings featured the account of a death resulting from a myopic posture of the membership. Although this story did not name the denomination, it did contain extensive details regarding the beginning, growth, decline, and ultimate end of a prominent church located in a small, midwestern town.

First Church of Greenville was established in 1845. For the first hundred years of its existence, the members worshipped in a wood frame building. With every pew packed it would hold 150 attendees, although it was rarely packed. On an average Sunday, around 50 individuals gathered for worship. Throughout its history, the church typically relied upon the services of a part-time or bi-vocational pastor. For some periods, First Church of Greenville shared their pastor with the First Church of Fairview, meeting only two Sundays a month for worship.

However, after the Second World War and the subsequent baby boom, Greenville experienced a substantial population growth. The small town of 2,000 residents grew to over 10,000 in under a decade. In the early 1950s, First Church hired its first full-time pastor to shepherd the more than 200 who attended each Sunday in multiple worship services. In 1955, the church made plans to construct a new worship center and Sunday School space on a parcel of property located just two blocks away from the old, nearly dilapidated, century-old sanctuary. The church members raised the necessary funds, hired an architect and contractor, and in 1961 moved to the brand-new campus of First Church. On the first Sunday of worship at this location, over 900 individuals somehow managed to pack out a worship center that sat only 800.

Throughout the 1960s, the church thrived. Most of the leading citizens of Greenville were members of First Church. Worship and Sunday School attendance was virtually mandatory. Unless one was seriously ill or out of town, members were expected to be in church on Sunday. Failure to do so brought judgmental stares and whispers of gossip about one's moral character. For example, an attorney who was absent for numerous Sundays without excuse would suddenly discover his clients seeking legal services from another attorney in town.

First Church's attendance and financial giving remained strong throughout the 1960s and 70s. In 1980, the church added a Family Life Center to its campus. This building hosted a basketball league in the fall and winter months and youth group activities throughout the year. First Church played a central role in the lives of many families in the small town of Greenville.

In the 1980s, though, the attendance in worship and Sunday School began to decline. The population of Greenville—which had boomed during the 1950s and 60s—began to stagnate in the 1970s. A manufacturing plant in town that had opened in 1949 closed its doors during the recession of the late 1970s. Children of the baby boomers moved to larger cities after high school or college. The population of Greenville and of First Church began to plateau and age. Worship attendees saw a graying of those seated in the pews around them.

In 1992, First Church hired a new pastor. The previous pastor, Dr. White, had retired in 1991 after faithfully serving the church for 34 years. He'd led the church in much of its growth and the move to their current campus. He officiated the weddings of most of the members of First Church and baptized almost everyone who sat in the pews on Sunday. He walked with families through tragedies and preached at more funerals than he could remember. The members of First Church greatly loved Dr. White; however, many in the church believed that he had remained as pastor about five years longer than necessary. The church that regularly had six or seven hundred in worship each Sunday in the 1960s saw half that number attend in the year before he retired. Moreover, the average age of the church had steadily increased. First Church was getting older and failing to add new members to its ranks.

The Pastor Search Committee strongly believed it needed to hire a younger pastor who could reach young families in the community. They extended a job offer to James Smith, 31, who served as a youth pastor at a larger church in Peoria, Illinois. James and his wife had two young children and were the perfect picture of the type of family First Church wanted to bring into their congregation.

The church warmly welcomed Mr. Smith and, in 1992, saw a steady increase in worship attendance. As much as the congregation loved Dr. White, his sermons were often slow, dry, and uninspiring. Mr. Smith brought a new style and a youthful energy to worship. He captured the attention of those present with his stories and application points. Through the end of 1992, Mr. Smith enjoyed what was called a "honeymoon stage" as the pastor of First Church.

In 1993, however, attitudes toward Mr. Smith shifted. This young pastor began making changes in the worship services at First Church. He asked an aging but beloved Minister of Music to retire and hired a younger individual who introduced a new style to their gatherings. Instead of leading from behind a pulpit and directing the congregation to sing from the hymnal, this young worship leader sat on a stool and played a guitar. The teenagers and a few younger couples in the congregation loved this innovative approach to worship, but the older members grumbled and complained. They wanted to sing the same songs they'd known for decades. Moreover, this new music person didn't exude the decorum and respect they thought appropriate for worship at First Church.

Mr. Smith also introduced new ways to engage families in the community. He changed the Sunday evening worship gathering and introduced elements that appealed to families with young children. Again, many members complained about this shift in the direction of the church. They wanted the church programming to remain intact.

According to some church members, Mr. Smith's list of inappropriate steps grew dramatically. Instead of wearing the accustomed coat and tie, Mr. Smith dressed more casually, wearing khaki pants and a golf shirt. He asked several church members to give up their Sunday morning Sunday School class to volunteer in the children's area. This pastor asked church members to assist him in going to visit those who were in the hospital. He canceled Sunday evening church to hold a class on how to do evangelism. All these changes weren't well received by the majority at First Church.

The straw that broke the camel's back was when Mr. Smith attempted to add a projector and screen to the church sanctuary so those in attendance could read and sing the lyrics to worship choruses. This change led to a business meeting where a member made a motion to ask for Mr. Smith's resignation.

According to the website:

> A 2/3 majority was necessary to remove the pastor. The vote was 301-149, just one vote more than what was required for the motion to pass. The chairman of the Personnel Team made a subsequent motion to offer the pastor two week's severance. It passed with nearly unanimous approval.

In August of 1995, Mr. Smith and a group of young families from First Church started "Greenville Community Church." They met in a local high school gym for two years, but the church didn't have the financial or human resources to successfully continue its operations. Eventually, the church dissolved, and Mr. Smith moved to another city.

First Church was left with a 20 percent decrease in its attendance. Most younger members left with Mr. Smith and then quit attending church altogether when Greenville Community Church disbanded.

In the 2000s and 2010s, the membership rolls and weekly worship numbers of First Church continued to decline. After the COVID pandemic of 2020, the fewer-than-fifty who gathered each Sunday rattled around in their 800-seat worship center. The church was only a few funerals away from closing its doors forever.

CALL TO ABANDON SELF?

Long before persecution from outside forces came against it, the American church was imploding from within. The First Church story became ubiquitous across the religious landscape of the United States. For the first two decades of the twenty-first century, every Christian denomination saw a significant decline in membership rolls, the only exception being a group called *The Assemblies of God*.[9] Throughout the country and spanning the range of theological beliefs and traditions, these internal battles led to congregants leaving their churches for good.

It seems quite ironic that this first thread became so prevalent in the American church. According to countless historical documents, the call of a Christian is to abandon self. I discovered numerous sources referencing quotes from the Bible urging Christians to do exactly that. For example:

- *Deny yourself daily.*
- *He who wants to be first must be last and a servant of all.*
- *Do not look out for your own interests, but also the interests of others.*
- *Humbly serve one another in love.*

These were only a few of the Christian teachings I discovered, all with the same theme: following Christ is a call to self-sacrifice. Christians, ideally, should place more emphasis on the needs of others before their own. The move away from this core tenet of Christianity became a major impetus to the decline of the American church.

However, it appears those who remained in many churches across the nation were willing to return to this fundamental principle of their faith. They were ready to heed the call of self-sacrifice once again. The bleeding of the membership rolls took a great toll on the American church; yet, it might have survived the decline in numbers if Christians had not abandoned another long-held belief and practice. There was the potential to recover and replace those who left these churches with new members. But the church faced yet another internal, detrimental change during this time. I cover this second thread of the church's death shroud in the next chapter.

CHAPTER 2

DON'T SPEAK

The Practical and Legal End of Evangelism

On the morning of January 31, 2049, Jonathan Thompson sat at a table in a quaint, cozy coffee shop in Lexington, Kentucky. Seated across from him was his friend, Bradley Moore. Both were, at the time, students at Lexington State University. Bradley and his girlfriend had recently split after a two-year relationship, and Bradley wanted to talk about everything that had recently transpired in his life. Jonathan was one of his few friends—someone he'd met during first-year orientation at LSU.

What Bradley didn't know—because Jonathan never told him—was that Jonathan was secretly a Christian. In the 2040s, there was tremendous social oppression against Christians, and nowhere more so than on most university campuses.

As well, Lexington State University had, five years earlier, instituted a strict policy against any speech which fell into the category of "religious persuasion." No one on campus was allowed, either in public forums or in private conversations, to use language that "intended to persuade another individual to embrace religious faith or practices."

This policy was modeled after a similar one instituted in 2039 at the University of the West in San Francisco, California. Almost immediately, this new UW rule was challenged as a violation of free speech. However, in the summer of 2040, the Supreme Court in *Watkins v California* agreed that a state entity could restrict speech in places where "young, impressionable minds may fall victim to philosophies and ideas incompatible with known realities."

Other college and university campuses, including Lexington State University, adopted similar policies. Students entering these colleges agreed to abide by these rules as a condition of their enrollment at the school. Public or private language explicitly used to coerce an individual or individuals into religious beliefs was expressively forbidden. Any violations of this policy would require the offender to appear before the Student Judicial Council and could result in expulsion from the school.

Up to this point in his college career, Jonathan had kept his faith private. However, when Bradley revealed that his recent romantic problems had left him feeling suicidal, Jonathan felt obligated to help. He shared with Bradley what he believed about God, Jesus, salvation, and finding purpose in life. Bradley listened intently, asked a few questions, and, after an hour of conversation, asked Jonathan how to become a Christian. The two friends quietly prayed together.

They returned to campus and—in his excitement over his conversion and this newfound philosophy of life—Bradley talked with several other individuals in his dorm about the events of that morning. News of Bradley's conversations with other students reached the Resident Advisor, who then shared the same information with the Dean of Students.

Both Bradley and Jonathan received notices requiring them to appear before the Judicial Council. Jonathan was expelled from the school. Bradley, as well. The school wanted to make an example out of these two students. Other minor infractions—casual comments about God, T-shirts with Christian language written on the front, Christian music played in a dorm room—had raised the ire of many students and faculty members. Even though Jonathan's infraction occurred off-campus and away from the jurisdiction of the Dean and the Judicial Council, the school wanted to send a clear message regarding its no-tolerance policy on persuasive speech. Bradley openly admitting that Jonathan's words led him to become a Christian was compelling evidence of why the policy existed and needed to be vigorously enforced.

This action sent a warning shot across the bow of the few remaining Christian college students at Lexington State University and other schools with similar speech policies. The point was clear: if you want to be accepted at our school and remain a student, keep your religious views to yourself.

Gone before It Was Illegal

Looking objectively at the history of these new university policies (as well, most corporations instituted similar rules in their personnel handbooks), this story has a strange irony. *Evangelism* is a word used by Christians to describe the sharing of their beliefs with others. The goal of evangelism is to convince the targeted individual to become a Christian. Throughout the church's history, this was viewed as a natural part of the Christian's life. Various writers of old described it as both an obligation and a privilege. Some argued that evangelism was as natural for Christians as swimming is for fish; sharing what their god had done for them was a byproduct of their changed life.

This was certainly true in the first two centuries of our nation's history. The number of Christians in the United States grew *steadily* and at times *quite rapidly* every decade from our founding until the 1980s. In the late 1970s, 90 percent of Americans identified as Christian.[10] This was due, in part, to the fact that church members faithfully evangelized and brought others into their ranks. Christians talked about their faith with non-Christians. As a result, membership rolls of the American church grew.

However, in the 1980s, church membership began to decline. By 2009, the number of Americans who identified as Christian dropped to 77 percent. Just ten years later, it fell another twelve points to 65 percent.[11] In 2029, only 42 percent of Americans claimed to be Christian. By 2039, under 15 percent of Americans openly accepted that label. This was the last year that this question was allowed in a survey. Today, the percentage of Americans who would admit to being Christian is minuscule.

For many years of our nation's history, the largest Protestant denomination in the United States was the Southern Baptist Convention. During the twentieth century, they saw a rapid growth in the number of churches in their denomination and their overall membership. The reason for their growth was due, in part, to their focus on evangelism. Most Southern Baptist churches emphasized the Christian's obligation to share their faith with those who were not Christian. From 1945 until 1995, this denomination grew exponentially, from approximately 5 million members to over 16 million.[12] This considerable growth directly resulted from a denomination that focused heavily on evangelism.

These outreach efforts remained strong until the latter part of the twentieth century. Around the turn of the millennium, however, members of these churches became reticent about sharing their faith. Many Christians viewed their religious beliefs as private matters, not to be discussed outside the church. This mindset shift made its way through all denominations, including the Southern Baptist Convention. These churches began seeing a slow decline in their baptism numbers (the primary way they measured their evangelistic success). By 2021, their baptisms had decreased by 65 percent from 1972, and this was during a time when the population of the nation was growing.[13] Moreover, the total membership of this denomination began declining as well, from 16 million to 13 million in 2020, 7 million in 2030, and only 2 million in 2039. Throughout the 2040s, the membership continued to decline, falling to just a few hundred thousand by the end of the decade.

Other Christian denominations saw an even more rapid decline. Christians once believed it was their obligation to talk with others about the Christian faith. Around the turn of the last century, though, this sense of responsibility among Christians had virtually disappeared.

Fewer and Fewer Shared Their Faith

In 2025, a Methodist pastor in Iowa posted his frustrations on a church leadership forum. That winter, his church offered three classes for adults on Sunday evenings to coincide with their youth and children's programming. One class was entitled "The Path to Financial Peace." The other was called "Understanding Your Temperament." The third was "How to Effectively Share Your Faith."

The pastor noted that 67 registered for the first class, 51 for the second, and only three signed up for the class on evangelism. This pastor wrote the following opinion about the lack of interest in the third Sunday evening offering:

> Maybe it's just that the first two classes were that intriguing, but even if they hadn't been offered, I don't think we would've had that many people sign up for a class on sharing your faith. I've sensed, more and more, that religious views are considered very private. Talking about one's faith in Christ has become akin to sharing details about one's bank account or 401(k) balances. Asking someone about their religious beliefs is as much a social faux pas as asking a lady about her weight.
>
> I remember when evangelism methods would begin with the question, "Have you accepted Jesus as your Lord and Savior?" This question then gave way to the more palatable, "If you died tonight, do you know where you would spend eternity?" This opening question was later softened even further by asking, "In your personal opinion, what does it take for someone to get to heaven?" I've noticed

that more recently written evangelism courses suggest beginning the discussion by asking, "Would you care to talk about spiritual things?" I imagine the next step down the ladder will be opening with, "How about this weather we're having?" and just hope the other person responds, "Can you tell me how to become a Christian?"

I've noticed that our church really isn't reaching anyone. And I don't think our church is alone in this. Unless Christians start acting like salt and light, churches everywhere will have to close their doors.

This pastor was correct. His church members certainly weren't the only ones not sharing their faith. On this same church forum, a recently retired pastor expressed his frustrations over the lack of outreach efforts by Christians in his later years of ministry. During the 1980s, his churches had a Tuesday night visitation virtually every week. A dozen or so met in the church fellowship hall at six o'clock and had dinner together. After dinner, they stood over maps of the city and made neighborhood assignments. Teams of 2-3 people would literally go door-to-door, knocking on doors and asking those who answered if they could share with them how to be saved.

Sometime in the 1990s—according to the pastor—this became a severely outdated form of evangelism. Many neighborhoods had entrances with gates, and a lot of people just wouldn't answer their door for a complete stranger. So, they started only visiting people who had some sort of connection with the church. Maybe they had visited the church; they called them "prospects." Or perhaps they had a child who played in the church's recreational basketball program. Or they were a friend or family member of a person in the church. Church members would still meet at the church on Tuesday nights, but most often, they would already have appointments arranged for that evening.

Eventually, the Tuesday night visitations fizzled out, and the church attempted new outreach methods. They became an "attractional" church, with excellent worship and programming, believing the Sunday morning offerings would be so compelling that they would attract non-believers. This seemed to work for a little while, but over time they discovered that non-believers just had so many other options; entertainment and sports and activities were far more "attractional" than their Sunday morning worship services. They continued to explore other methods of sharing the gospel; however, most members simply weren't interested in personally discussing their faith with non-Christians. This retired pastor expressed frustration over the ever-diminishing desire of church members to do any kind of evangelism:

> We've got the greatest message in the world in the gospel! We should be like a doctor who has discovered the cure for cancer, busting to tell the world about this wonderful answer to our spiritual disease. Instead, we guard it like a bunch of Masons concealing the elements of their secret ritual. More than music, preaching, or our discipleship programs, the incredible silence about our faith is the biggest change I have seen during my lifetime in church ministry.

The de-emphasis on evangelism was a common theme in the American church during this period. Sharing one's religious views became passé among Christians. Discussions about politics, sports, and the economy were all much more common and socially acceptable.

A Slow-But-Steady Death

In 1988, Calvary Church in Pennsylvania constructed a new 800-seat worship center. Even with multiple services, this space was comfortably full on most Sundays and uncomfortably full on Easter and other high-attendance days. Throughout the 1980s and 90s, Calvary was a healthy, growing, thriving church in its community.

However, around the turn of the century, the church plateaued. In less than a decade, the stagnation turned to decline. The falling numbers were slow and steady for about ten years but dropped off steeply after the pandemic of 2020. In 2026, the pastor and church leaders decided to seek counsel from an outside source. They contacted a ministry called *Church Growth Solutions* and spent six months in conversations with two consultants from this organization. The church leaders were then presented with a written report analyzing the strengths and weaknesses of the church. One section of this evaluation was particularly enlightening:

> For decades, the members of Calvary believed they were responsible for the church's ministry. They invited neighbors and friends who were unchurched. They were intentional about relational evangelism. In 1991, for example, the church averaged 1,581 in weekend worship. That same

year, the church baptized 152 individuals. It took approximately ten church attendees to win one person to faith.

In 2012, the average weekend worship was 1,134, and 29 individuals were baptized (note: 25 were under eighteen years old). That year, it took nearly 40 attendees to see one person come to faith in Christ.

The reason behind this change is that church members lost a sense of ownership at some point in the late 90s or early 2000s. The church grew to the point that they hired professionals to carry out the work of the ministry, including evangelism. Most members showed up on Sundays and heard excellent music performed by talented professionals. They listened to another professional present a well-crafted message. Some gave financially, others simply listened and left. They no longer felt obligated to engage in the ministry.

We surveyed every Calvary member and discovered that only 1 in 100 had discussed their religious beliefs with a non-Christian in the previous year. Calvary's decline hasn't occurred because of a scandal or division within the church. Rather, the church simply hasn't replaced itself. As members have either moved or passed away, there haven't been new ones to take their place. Without a mindset change, we believe Calvary will continue to decline by 40-60 attendees each year, meaning that the church will most likely close its doors in 2039.

Calvary is just one example of thousands of churches with similar stories. In 2028, a study of Protestant churches in North

Carolina revealed that it took 325 church members per annual baptism, including the baptisms of children who were already in the church. During the first part of the 21st century, most churches throughout the United States became exclusive clubs, closed to outsiders—so much so that when, in the 2040s, restrictions on evangelism became widespread throughout America, evangelism had already died. For over twenty years prior, Christians no longer talked about their faith anyway. These new laws simply codified what was already an existing reality.

The Strange Irony

Throughout the 40s, numerous legal challenges were made to the various policies and laws restricting religious language. The religious liberties guaranteed by the First Amendment, it was said, represent the very core of democracy. The Constitution would never have been ratified without the inclusion of the Bill of Rights, and there is a good reason that religious freedom is mentioned first in this document. The founders of our nation, Christians asserted, understood well the dangers of a nation persecuting religious views. Many of the early settlers who first landed on the shores of this new nation came here specifically in search of religious freedom.

Ultimately, though, these assertions did not persuade the majority opinion in our nation. Those same founders, it was noted, also believed slavery was an acceptable institution. Any argument based on the intent of these white, privileged individuals must also recognize the historical fact of their abhorrent, twisted thinking.

The reality that all the founders' images have been removed from our modern currency testifies to our culture's recognition of their immoral treatment of millions in our nation. While they boldly proclaimed, "that all men are created equal and are endowed... with certain unalienable rights," they shamelessly restricted the rights of the enslaved. Simply put, one cannot demand that the rights guaranteed in the Constitution should be universally applied when they've not always been universally applied.

Moreover, the freedom of religion and speech can only extend to the point that both do not endanger the lives of others. Americans have the freedom of speech, for example, but not the freedom to falsely yell "fire" in a crowded theater and risk harming those who are present.

The overwhelming majority of the American population agrees with the restrictions on religious language used for the purpose of persuasion. If someone foolishly chooses to believe in myths and non-corporal beings, that is certainly their right. But, they cannot attempt to indoctrinate others with these ideas. Across the nation, regulations against written and verbal religious communication have been welcomed. No one should be coerced into believing that which goes against known facts.

However, there is a strange paradox in the story of the American church. While Christians bemoaned the institutional and governmental restrictions on religious language, these laws and policies would have never been enacted if Christians hadn't given up on their evangelistic efforts. Schools and corporations felt the freedom to impose rules against religious speech largely because they knew there would be few objections. The number of Christians in our nation declined to the point that the voices of this small minority weren't very loud. These restrictions affected very few.

In other words, because they didn't share their faith, Christians could no longer share their faith.

At the same time churches saw an evangelistic atrophy among their membership, another change brought about a tremendous reduction in Sunday morning worship attendance. I cover this widespread cultural phenomenon in the next chapter.

CHAPTER 3

JESUS, JUST ANOTHER OPTION

How Busyness Weakened the Church

F or most of our nation's history, Sunday was considered a day of rest. Besides attending church and visiting relatives, not much else happened on this first day of the week. Only police, firefighters, medical personnel, and other essential service providers worked on Sundays. Virtually all commercial businesses closed. Recreational sports teams did not play or practice. Church attendance was the central Sunday activity for most Americans.

On an archived blog, a writer described their childhood growing up in the 1970s:

> When I was a teenager, our family would go "visiting" on Sunday afternoons. Visiting meant we went to see grandparents, uncles, or cousins. Sometimes, when we went to my Uncle Robert's house, it was fun. My two cousins and I would play football in the yard or explore the woods while my parents and the other adults sat around and talked. But when we went to my grandparents' house, there was no

one to play with. I was bored. My parents and grandparents would visit for hours, and I was expected to entertain myself.

To make matters worse, my grandfather had a pond stocked full of catfish, bream, bass, and crappie. I loved fishing in that pond, and he said I could do it anytime. Except Sundays. I remember asking him, "Grandpa, why can't I fish on Sundays?"

"Because Sundays are a day of rest."

"But Grandpa, fishing is relaxing to me. It's not work."

"Yeah, but it's work for the fish. *No fishing on Sundays.*"

For me, Sundays were often not a day of rest but a day of complete boredom.

This individual's account of their childhood Sundays wasn't unique for this period in American history. The notion that Sundays were a sabbath was a commonly held belief. Commercial and recreational options were severely limited on the first day of the week. When deciding between "going to church" or some other activity, most people had no other choice. There were few other offerings to interfere with worship services and Sunday School classes.

But, in the early part of the twenty-first century, a new threat invaded the church. It was slow and subtle. Unlike the fights described in the first chapter, this particular peril was quiet. There were no debates or long business meetings. This issue didn't lead directly to a pastor's termination or angry emails sent to church board members. Most Christians barely noticed this enemy of the church. That is, until it was too late. It was this specific aspect of American life that dealt one of the deadliest blows to the church.

We're Not Mad, Just Busy!

From the founding of this nation until the 1980s and 90s, Christians often found their social lives revolving around church and church activities. Retail stores and business closed their doors on Sundays. School and community sports teams did not play or practice on Sunday. Since many churches held mid-week services on Wednesdays, recreational sports leagues avoided hosting games on Wednesday evenings.

During the last years of the twentieth century, however, a noticeable shift happened in most communities across the United States. Sundays were no longer sacrosanct. The busyness of culture required a full two days on the weekends to incorporate all the desired activities of the average family. Most stores were open on Sundays, requiring Christians working in these businesses to forgo church in order to earn a paycheck. Various entertainment venues—previously closed on Sundays—began to mirror their Saturday hours of operation. In most communities, life on a Sunday morning looked and felt like Saturday. Traffic on roads, congestion in stores and restaurants, and leisure activities all reflected the move away from Sundays being a "sabbath" day. Church attendance and rest were no longer priorities for many Americans.

Families were particularly impacted when recreational leagues began scheduling Sunday morning games. If a child wanted to play a certain sport, the family had to choose between that activity and church attendance. The option of playing at a high level without being required to participate in Sunday games was no longer available. Christian parents often felt forced into a less-than-ideal situation. They wanted their child to succeed in a particular sport, yet they also felt like their child needed to attend church. Many personal blogs of these parents referenced the old adage of "feeling stuck between a rock and a hard place."

The culture's changing approach to Sundays dramatically impacted church attendance. Recreational sports had a particularly detrimental effect on Sunday worship gatherings. I found an entire thread devoted to this topic on an archived church leaders' discussion board. Pastors lamented the fact that a family would be absent most Sundays because their child played in weekend competitions. Commonly, tennis and baseball tournaments required a family to travel to another city and sit through a full day of Saturday and Sunday matches and games. A congregation with only four or five children or teenagers involved in these weekend sporting events could potentially experience a decrease in worship attendance by 20-25 individuals. Moms, Dads, and siblings would all be away from Sunday School and church to attend the weekend tournament.

Forced to Choose

By 2025, Sundays were virtually indistinguishable from Saturdays across the United States. Businesses, restaurants, recreational sports leagues, and entertainment venues offered the same hours as on Saturday. Only a few decades earlier, many of those same cities and towns had what was known as "Blue Laws," regulations against certain businesses opening on Sundays and, more commonly, restrictions against the sale of alcohol on Sundays.

Those days were long gone.

Numerous blogs from this time described the angst experienced by parents who felt as if they had no choice in the matter. If their child wanted to play sports at a competitive level, they had to participate in weekend tournaments. It was impossible to remain committed to one's church and to the athletic successes of one's child. For those children and teenagers who possessed enough talent to possibly play at the collegiate level, weekend tournaments were a requirement. This was where teenagers expected to get noticed by college athletic recruiters.

In a parenting blog from 2026, one parent wrote about moving to Springfield and joining Lakeside Methodist Church. She and her husband volunteered with the youth, mainly by teaching a small group and going on retreats. When they had their first child, he was dedicated at the church. With a newborn keeping them in town and homebound on most weekends, they were rarely absent from church on Sundays. Her husband served on the leadership board. She volunteered in the preschool. As this writer described it, they were a family that was "all-in" at Lakeside.

But, just a few years later, her son started playing tennis at four years old and absolutely loved it. The coach at the recreation department said he was a natural. He took lessons once a week, then twice a week, and gradually tennis practice became an everyday-after-school activity. He started playing in USTA tournaments and winning most of his matches. His coaches pushed these parents to sign him up for more tournaments, but this meant giving up their weekends to travel to other cities. And it meant missing church on Sunday.

They were absent so many Sundays that, eventually, they resigned from their volunteer positions at the church. On the few weekends their son didn't have a tennis tournament, they would go to worship as a family. But there would be so many new people, they felt like were strangers, looking in on a place that had once been their spiritual home.

As well, when they were in town, her son didn't enjoy going to church. He felt like he didn't fit in and had no friends. So, they didn't push the issue, especially since they were home so few weekends. They did everything they could to support him in his tennis career.

Then, everything changed. On her blog, this mom wrote:

> Last year, he suddenly and unexpectedly announced that he was done with tennis. He'd lost a couple of matches the previous weekend and seemed discouraged, but evidently, some angst had been building in him for a while. We tried and tried to change his mind, all but forcing him to play. But he dug in his heels and would not budge. His tennis career was over.
>
> Now, he's a first-year student in college, NOT playing tennis, and has zero interest in church. We had some good times together, but looking back now, I don't know. Our tennis ambitions stole our church from us.

In multiple ways, church members were forced to choose between attendance at worship gatherings and other obligations. Numerous jobs and careers required working on Sundays. Individuals sometimes had to choose between employment and church. Events and gatherings increasingly happened on Sunday mornings. Most in the community considered this an open time slot on the calendars of an incredibly busy culture. Christians were expected to forgo Sunday morning worship gatherings for these other obligations.

Unlike the myopic stage, members in the apathy stage weren't mad at the church or pastors. They generally had favorable views toward the church's programs and leaders. They even gave financially to the church (although in decreasing percentages of their income over the years). An average member might attend only ten Sundays a year and yet consider themselves active, committed church members. They went to worship services sporadically, gave infrequently, and rarely served. Yet, the church was still very much, "their church."

NO ONE IS HERE, BUT NO ONE LEFT

This trend had two noticeable effects on the health of churches. One was a significant decline in worship attendance, even though members had not left the church. Individuals and families who formerly attended three times a month attended only once a month. When numerous families in a church fell into this same pattern, overall worship attendance declined, sometimes dramatically. A church accustomed to seeing 200 people in Sunday morning worship suddenly saw its attendance fall into the low 100's without any significant, identifiable issue causing the drop. Church leaders were often left scratching their heads, wondering why their numbers were down when no one had "left the church."

I discovered an archived PDF written by the pastor of Christ Community Church in Texas detailing this trend for the church's elder board. The document contained statistics from the 2026-27 church year. The church had eight more baptisms than the previous year, and the church membership roll grew by twenty. Yet, the overall attendance had declined by more than 10 percent, which had been the trend for the last several years. In a narrative describing the "State of the Church," the pastor explained this somewhat odd paradox:

> In the last five years, there have been no significant departures from the church. Other than the few families who have moved away and the deaths of a couple of long-time church members, no one has left. There certainly haven't been any issues causing a mass exodus of congregants. Moreover, in the last five years, we've reached over 75 new individuals who have joined or become regular attendees at Christ Community.
>
> And yet, our overall attendance is down by 30 percent compared to five years ago, and we were still "coming out of COVID" that year! The only explanation is that our members do not come as often. A family that once attended four Sundays a month is now only coming three. Three-a-monthers are now coming twice a month. Two-ers now come once a month. Those who only came once a month come every other month. Amazingly, though, most of these individuals and families consider themselves active and committed. It's just that everyone is so busy with other things!

This decline in worship attendance was typical in virtually every Christian denomination and across every region of the country.

The second noticeable effect was a strain on churches to maintain programs. Those who had once been committed volunteers now had other obligations. This meant individuals and families visiting these churches for the first time saw understaffed programs. The church that had formerly offered excellent Sunday morning preschool lessons and care could now barely procure one or two volunteers to babysit children while their parents went to church. Across these churches, ministries became severely understaffed. While members gladly attended worship when their schedules permitted, few were able to make commitments to teaching and serving in other capacities. Thus, the quality of programming in these churches deteriorated, sometimes quite severely.

This reality had a downward spiral effect on churches: members were absent, creating an environment where it was difficult to attract new members to replace the absentees. The busyness of church members led to many formerly healthy, thriving churches becoming unhealthy and only fractions of what they had once been.

No Way Back

When the persecution of the church intensified during the 2030s and 40s, many of those formerly absentee members returned. Ironically, even though they rarely attended worship, they held a strong allegiance to "their church." For many, their grandparents and great-grandparents had been members of these houses of worship. Even though their own attendance was sporadic at best, they wanted to defend their church and their right to gather for worship.

However, the church had become so weakened by this point that these efforts were of little consequence. Christians were the definite minority in our culture and had little standing or influence in most communities.

An archived blog entitled *The Secret Christian* contained the following undated entry:

> For years, church attendance wasn't a priority for our family. We went when it was convenient. If we were up late on Saturday, we would tell our son and daughter, "We need to sleep in and spend tomorrow getting ready for the week ahead. We'll go next Sunday." Often, we were out of town on the weekends and unable to go. Or just busy with other things. My wife and I often talked about how we would "get back into it" when our kids graduated from high school and life wasn't so busy.
>
> Then, about the time our kids went off to college, going to church became hard. My company began to keep a watchful eye on anyone who attended church gatherings. We were required to participate in classes called "Equality in the Workplace" and sign "tolerance pledges." I knew I had to choose: keep my job and support my wife and college-aged kids or go public about my Christian beliefs. I decided to remain quiet. I had way too many financial obligations. I just couldn't risk it.
>
> Looking back, I wish I'd been more active in church when it didn't cost so much. I just took for granted that church would be there, waiting for me when I was finally

ready to return. I didn't realize how great we had it when we were free to worship without persecution.

Although subtle, this new phenomenon did tremendous damage to the church in America. Pastors and other leaders complained, but very few offered solutions. Most shrugged their shoulders and scratched their heads, unable to find answers. This was now the new normal of our culture. Individuals and families were just way too busy for faithful worship attendance, adding tremendously to the decline of the American church.

The myopic stage of the church and the apathetic stage both significantly weakened the church. However, the next phase attacked its very foundation, leaving the church in a place where it was unable to survive the coming persecution.

CHAPTER 4

NOT YOUR GRANDDAD'S BIBLE

Progressive Churches Attempt to Adapt

For most of the church's history, certain fundamental beliefs defined the word *Christian*. The following truths were considered to be foundational tenets of Christianity:

- There is one god (God) who created the universe and is omniscient, omnipresent, and perfect.
- All humans are born separated from this god because of their "sin" nature. Sin is the violation of this god's law in word, thought, or deed. This nature is passed down from parents to children.
- This god is "holy." Holiness is the state of complete perfection. Therefore, the sin of humans creates a chasm between them and this god.
- No good works or religious actions can bridge the gap between any person and this god.

- Jesus came as this god in human form, although separate and distinct from this god. Paradoxically, he was also one-in-the-same with this god.
- Jesus was born of a virgin birthing-person. Therefore, he didn't inherit this sinful nature.
- Jesus lived a perfect life but was put to death and received the punishment for the sins of humans.
- Jesus rose from the dead, thus demonstrating his power over physical death and sin.
- All humans who trust in Jesus will find their sins forgiven, realize a relationship with this god, and receive the promise of life after death in a place called heaven.

Christians traditionally held to these ideas as essential truths of their faith. A rejection of one or more of these concepts generally excluded one from the church. One could not deny the resurrection of Jesus, for example, and still claim the title "Christian." These were the foundational, minimal beliefs necessary for salvation and admittance into the Christian church.

Certainly, Christians possessed differing beliefs regarding secondary and tertiary issues. Churches used varying forms of governance throughout the numerous Christian denominations. They disagreed over how they should practice worship. They held different views about a subject called "eschatology," or teachings on the end of the world.

As well, significant divisions occurred over the issue of baptism. Baptism is a Christian practice in which an individual is "initiated" with water into their group. Some churches believed this initiation could be accomplished by sprinkling water on the head, others practiced pouring the baptismal water over the individual, and still, others insisted this water initiation must involve pushing new converts completely underwater, an exercise which sounds slightly sadistic to our modern ears.

There were disagreements on other subordinate matters; however, Christians generally held to those main tenets as outlined above. At our nation's founding, Baptists, Methodists, Presbyterians, Quakers, Catholics, and other Christian groups agreed on these "fundamentals of the faith." Those who disagreed with these tenets, by definition, could not rightly be called "Christian."

The Gospel according to an Atheist

Christopher Hitchens was an eloquent, learned atheist who fought vigorously against religious ideas in general and Christianity in particular. During his lifetime, Mr. Hitchens did much to advance the views of Americans and Great Britains on the absurdities of the Christian faith. His book, *God Is Not Great: How Religion Poisons Everything*, identified the dangers of organized religion and helped readers understand the personal perils of imaginative, unprovable beliefs. Mr. Hitchens often debated Christian leaders and appeared in numerous forums devoted to the examination of religious ideas and their effects on society.

Two years before his death in 2011, Hitchens was interviewed by Marilyn Sewell, a minister in the Unitarian church. The discussion centered on the content of his book, *God Is Not Great*. Ms. Sewell noted that the book criticized what she described as a "fundamentalist faith." She then explained that her own beliefs were quite different from this brand of Christianity. For example, she did not believe in the traditional doctrine of atonement—that Jesus died for the sins of humanity. She then asked Mr. Hitchens, "Do you make a distinction between fundamentalist faith and [my] liberal religion?"

Much to the surprise of Ms. Sewell, his answer was, "Well, I would say that if you don't believe that Jesus of Nazareth was the Christ and Messiah, and that he rose again from the dead and by his sacrifice our sins are forgiven, you're really not in any meaningful sense a Christian."[14]

Hitchens himself very much did not believe that Jesus was the Messiah and that he rose again from the dead. His books focused primarily on disproving this assertion and other claims of Christians. He debated and belittled those who agreed with the doctrine of the atonement. Christopher Hitchens was an evangelistic atheist—one who vigorously sought to win others to his system of beliefs and worldview.

However, Hitchens understood well the Christian scriptures and the traditional teachings of the church. A gospel without the doctrine of the atonement is a logical contradiction. Either Jesus is the Messiah and the way for individuals to find forgiveness of sin, or he is not. Christianity rises or falls on this "fundamental" of the faith. A third way—Christianity without Jesus as the source of salvation—is inconsistent with the Bible and the historical beliefs of the church.

Quite ironically, an atheist pointed out the fallacy of claiming to be a Christian while denying the atoning work of Jesus. Can one claim to be a Muslim, yet completely reject the teachings of Mohammad? Does it make sense to call oneself a Marxist, but express complete disagreement with the teachings of Karl Marx? Can a politician who believes in lower taxes, limited government, and the supposed "rights" of a fetus rightly be called a Democrat?

Similarly, there are foundational beliefs necessary for one to accurately be called, "Christian." To remove these doctrines steals the essence of this religion.

That fact, however, didn't keep some from trying.

"Saving" Christianity

Beginning in the late nineteenth century, a theological shift occurred in the American church. These new ideas were initially called *liberal theology*, and then later adopted the label *Progressive Christianity*. Sometime shortly after the American Civil War, these new teachings wormed their way into institutions of higher learning. While these beliefs had various nuances, they essentially deemphasized sin, judgment, and repentance. At the heart of this movement was the rejection of the fundamental beliefs about original sin, the virgin birth, salvation through Jesus alone, and the resurrection.

The argument from many academics was that for Christianity to remain relevant in the world of higher education, Christian beliefs needed to adapt to secular, humanistic teachings. This new brand of Christianity, they asserted, would be more palatable to those with a scientific view of the world. The miracles of Jesus (and other miracles throughout the Bible) were placed under a microscope and given logical explanations. The proponents of a revised Christianity highlighted the teachings of Jesus as a good moral code while deemphasizing his divine nature.

J. Gresham Machen was a professor at Princeton University, a school founded by the protestant denomination called "Presbyterians." When Princeton began incorporating liberal theology into its curriculum in the early 1900s, Dr. Machen vigorously fought against this new teaching. He asserted that "The chief modern rival of Christianity is 'liberalism.' An examination of the teachings of liberalism in comparison with those of Christianity will show that at every point the two movements are in direct opposition."[15]

However, Machen was unsuccessful in this battle. This liberal theology found a welcoming home not only at Princeton, but also in many other universities and seminaries. Pastors trained at these schools began to teach this same theology in their sermons and lectures. Branches of Baptist, Presbyterian, Methodist, Episcopal, Lutheran, and other denominations incorporated these beliefs into their various creeds and statements of faith, although not always with certain clarity and agreement among their members. Generally, these churches disregarded sin, judgment, the need for repentance, hell (a non-Christian's so-called place for eternal judgment), and other less culturally acceptable teachings of the church. Jesus was no longer considered the way to salvation; instead, he became a model for how we should live our lives. Being kind to one another, helping the poor, and fighting for social justice became hallmarks of these churches.

This was, in many ways, an attempt to "save" Christianity. They believed that only through changing core theological beliefs would Christianity survive in a more modern, scientific world. By redefining what it means to be *Christian*, they argued, churches would open wide their doors, welcoming those who previously shunned the church because of what they considered old-fashioned, narrow-minded beliefs.

LIBERAL THEOLOGY 2.0: PROGRESSIVE CHRISTIANITY

In the early 2000s, Progressive Christians argued a similar case. This iteration, however, focused less on theological beliefs and more on the Christian moral code. By this time in our nation's history, our society's views on marriage had changed significantly. The *Obergefell v. Hodges* Supreme Court case of 2015 solidified this public sentiment. Same-sex marriage was defined as a constitutional right. States were no longer allowed to deny marriage licenses to homosexual couples. The definition of marriage had broadened considerably, and the church had to face this new reality.

Those in the Progressive Christian segment of the American church embraced this new concept of marriage. This adaptation to culture, it was again argued, would save the church. Individuals could hold the same views as the rest of society (especially on the issues of sex and marriage) yet still find a place of worship and community in the church. Many congregations adopted this LGBTQ+ friendly stance in hopes of growing the population of their congregations.

The logic went something like the following:

- Society believes that same-sex partnerships are morally acceptable and equivalent to "traditional" marriage.

- We should not only welcome those individuals with same-sex relationships into our churches but affirm their lifestyle choices as acceptable within the code of Christian ethics.
- This will open the doors of our church much wider. Our beliefs will align with culture; therefore, Christianity will not be objectionable to those around us.
- Removing these barriers will result in more people joining our congregation.
- This transition will ultimately save Christianity (or, more particularly, *our church*) from the trash heap of history.

An archived blog from a church in Georgia outlined their process of deciding to fully include LGBTQ+ individuals in the life of their congregation, along with the anticipated result of this decision. The undated article included the following (bold type added by this researcher):

In May of 2017, church leadership voted to recommend that the church fully include all people, regardless of sexual orientation or gender identity, in the life of the church, and to allow same-sex marriages to be performed in the church sanctuary...Members acknowledged their fears that people they loved might leave, or that the church would be perceived differently, **but they also lifted up their hopes that a *yes* vote would mean more people might be able to find a church that affirmed their full identities.**[16]

In the years surrounding the *Obergefell* decision, many other congregations across the United States also voted to revise their stance on the inclusion of LGBTQ+ individuals in the life of the church and to allow clergy to perform same-sex marriage ceremonies. For many, this became a litmus test for those inquiring about a congregation. *Are you LGBTQ+ inclusive or not? Do you affirm LGBTQ+ sexual choices as morally acceptable within the code of Christian ethics?* Other characteristics of the church—worship style, missions involvement, beliefs about baptism—all took a secondary position to this defining issue.

The question that lingered for many (both inside and outside these now LGBTQ+ inclusive congregations) was this: *Would these churches now attract more people?* Would a *yes* vote on inclusion mean, as the writer above expressed, more people might be able to find a church that affirmed their full identities? Would those who objected to the countercultural teachings of traditional churches now desire to join with these Progressive Christian congregations, causing these churches to significantly grow their membership rolls?

In 2030, the *Hatcher Group* (at the time, a leading researcher of religious life in America), surveyed two hundred churches that had transitioned to becoming LGBTQ+ inclusive sometime between 2015 and 2025. This study revealed a 43 percent decline in the average worship attendance of these churches within three years after this change in policy. Ironically, this change had the opposite effect of what many church leaders had hoped would be the case. Those who disagreed with the new stance on marriage left the church, and very few others came to backfill this void. While the culture's view of these churches was generally more favorable than its view of conservative churches, it didn't lead to more individuals joining these so-called "inclusive" or "affirming" congregations. A researcher from Hatcher made the following conclusion regarding these findings:

> While the "why" behind this phenomenon is still being studied, early research indicates that most outsiders are not attracted to a church that mirrors the values of the culture. They happily wish the church the best and will speak positively about the church. If an affirming church sponsors a community event, for example, these individuals would not protest their involvement like they would if a non-affirming church were to sponsor it. Even so, these individuals have little desire to invest their time or money in an organization that differs little from civic groups and other organizations within their community. In essence, these churches offered nothing substantially different from the culture; therefore, the average person saw little or no value in joining its membership.

The trend noted by the Hatcher Group in 2030 continued over the coming years. The 2030s became known as the decade of church closings. More churches dissolved during those ten years than in any other decade in the history of the American church. Scores of congregations were forced to close their doors simply because they were no longer able to financially maintain their facilities. In certain communities, particularly in the Northeast and the Pacific Northwest, there were literally no church buildings used for congregational worship. Those who wanted to attend a church worship service had to drive to the next town or to a larger city to find a gathering of

Christians. Many opted to remain at home and watch online worship services streamed from across the country and the world. There became fewer and fewer options for "going to church" in a traditional fashion. The closings of these "progressive" churches contributed significantly to the new reality of religious life in America.

In 2028, a former pastor of a progressive congregation wrote about the change in her church to becoming an "affirming congregation." In 2017, after a two-year study committee presented its findings, the church voted to allow same-sex weddings in their sanctuary and to allow their clergy to officiate same-sex ceremonies both on and off their campus. Following is how she reflected on that watershed moment in the life of this church:

> The vote was 296-134. I remember those numbers well because the next year, 2018, our Sunday morning average attendance declined by 136. It didn't take a rocket scientist to figure out why those people left!
>
> However, we held out hope that others would come and take their place. Our newly stated policy would appeal to others in our community, right? I and other church leaders sincerely believed 2019 would be the year our church really started to grow.
>
> But it didn't.
>
> Then COVID hit in 2020.
>
> When we finally "regathered" in 2021, all wearing our masks, there were far fewer faces. It was clear that many church members weren't coming back. Attendance continued to decline over the next few years.

I remember the Sunday morning I looked out at the congregation and saw that we actually had fewer people in the pews than we did in the choir, and there were only ten in the choir! Our old, beautiful, very traditional sanctuary could hold nearly 800 worshippers. Some of the old-timers at the church talked about the days when it was full most Sundays. I can't imagine. As I looked around at the gray hair of those few eyes staring back at me, I knew the end was coming soon.

Numerous other affirming churches had similar experiences. Many were part of mainline congregations and, like the church described above, had a long history in the community and old, aging facilities in great need of repair. Some churches had endowments that enabled them to renovate and, most often, decrease the size of their sanctuaries to more adequately reflect their reduced attendance. Other congregations did not fare as well. I found over two dozen articles referencing historic churches having to sell their properties simply because they could not afford to maintain their campuses. The decline in their numbers meant the churches no longer needed the space, anyway, so why spend money to maintain the property? This combination of low attendance and expensive buildings prompted the end of numerous progressive churches.

The change in theology was one factor in the decline of the church. However, other congregations found themselves caught in the LGBTQ+ quandary unintentionally. These were not liberal churches. In fact, most considered themselves to be evangelical and conservative. Yet, they were not properly prepared to face the sea change of morals in the culture.

In the next chapter, we will see how these churches unwittingly fell victim to the pressures from society and their own memberships.

CHAPTER 5

DR. PHIL, OPRAH, AND JESUS

How Theological Shallowness
Weakened the Church

In the 1990s, a relatively new brand of Christianity began dotting America's religious landscape. Over the course of a couple of decades, our nation experienced an explosion of non-traditional church plants. While most major Protestant denominations saw declines in attendance and membership, many of these non-traditional churches grew rapidly. They were influenced by churches like Saddleback Church in California, Willow Creek Community Church in Chicago, and Life Church in Oklahoma City, Oklahoma. Most had a contemporary style of music and a casual, "come-as-you-are" atmosphere. They purposefully appealed to the non-churched person in their worship styles and messages. The person unfamiliar with religious rituals and who did not own a Christian Bible purportedly felt welcome in these churches.

The majority of these churches held traditional, orthodox Christian beliefs. They explained these beliefs on their websites and in new member's classes. They discussed their views on

God, Jesus, the Holy Spirit, the Bible, and salvation. Some of these churches, however, shied away from specific teachings on secondary issues such as divorce or beliefs about creation and the end times. As well, a number of these churches left their stance on LGBTQ+ inclusion ambiguous. This avoidance of hot-button issues, for some, stemmed from their desire to place most of their emphasis on the practical affairs of everyday life. They focused on the Bible's teachings about handling worry, money, relationships, and other matters considered relevant for the here and now. Two then-popular television talk shows, *Dr. Phil* and *Oprah,* focused on similar topics: how individuals can improve their lives by changing their mindsets and behavior. Many compared the teachings in some non-traditional churches to the content on these television shows.

For years, most churches of this kind existed and thrived without significant problems. Millions of individuals found a spiritual home in these congregations. Many of these churches were known for excellence in their worship production and programming. A weekend worship service typically featured incredibly talented (and often well-paid) musicians. Their venues contained the latest technology of their day, including laser projectors, LED screens, moving lights, and haze machines to add a certain ambiance to the room.

The pastor was almost always a great communicator. Often, this was their primary focus. Members of these non-traditional churches didn't expect the pastor to be available for individual care. Most of these pastors did little in the way of counseling, hospital visitation, or other personally directed ministry. Congregants understood and accepted this reality. Very few who attended these churches desired a relationship with their pastor.

Rather, they expected to show up on a Sunday morning and hear a well-crafted, highly applicable message from this individual.

The worship services typically featured thirty minutes of excellent, professionally performed music with extremely talented vocalists. Then, the pastor would deliver a message centered on a present need of most in the congregation. *How to Handle Worry, Six Steps to A Healthy Marriage, Finding Financial Freedom, and Navigating the Teenage Years* were all examples of sermon titles found on archived websites from these non-traditional churches.

As well, many of these churches held Christmas, Easter, and Fourth of July programs that would attract thousands from the community. One such church in South Carolina hosted an annual July 4th tribute at a nearby college's football stadium. Each year, nearly 10,000 people from the community attended this highly publicized event. The program featured patriotic songs, recognition of veterans, well-produced videos, and live drama. The church spent thousands of man-hours and just as many dollars on this annual performance.

A non-denominational megachurch in Texas held an annual Christmas production in its large worship center. The event became so popular in the community that the church sold tickets to those wishing to attend. The multiple performances raised millions of dollars to both offset the cost of the elaborate production and to help support the church budget.

Generally, this brand of Christianity strongly believed that their worship gatherings, productions, ministries, marketing, and all other aspects of church life should be done with a high degree of excellence. Often, highly skilled musicians were paid to lead worship services, even though these individuals were not professing Christians. Talent mattered more than character or beliefs. These churches viewed themselves as competing with a culture that both expected and delivered high-quality productions. Children's ministry programming rivaled the secular entertainment industry. Videos used in worship gatherings possessed the caliber of a Hollywood movie. *If we expect people to choose church over culture*, the logic went, *then everything we offer must be done with excellence.*

SECRETLY CONSERVATIVE

Interestingly, these churches were generally considered "orthodox" in their view of God, Jesus, and the authority of Scripture. While some non-traditional churches taught these truths in their worship and small groups, many decided to focus their teachings on what they considered to be the more relevant, immediate needs of their members. As referenced above, they examined the Bible's teachings on money, relationships, anxiety, and other struggles common to the human experience. It wasn't that these churches had *unorthodox* theology; they just had *very little* theology.

For the first two decades of this century, these churches managed to avoid taking a stand on the more controversial issues brewing in the culture at the time. They didn't discuss, for example, same-sex marriage or the difference between *accepting individuals* and *affirming* their lifestyle choices. When asked, many of these churches offered vague responses such as, "Everyone is welcome and loved in our church." The lack of clarity allowed the churches to grow without offending those on either side of this divisive issue.

However, in the 2020s, this was no longer an option. Churches and denominations realized that they had to clearly communicate their beliefs regarding same-sex marriage and gender fluidity. Corporations, municipalities, media outlets, and the culture in general had, in the previous decade, shifted their views of what was considered to be morally right and wrong. Same-sex marriage, for example, was regarded by the majority of the American population to be an acceptable practice. As well, the culture recognized gender fluidity and made accommodations for these individuals. Schools and businesses gave strict guidelines on personal pronoun usage. Individuals were allowed to use public restrooms correlating with their gender identity rather than the gender assigned at their birth. Biological males who had transitioned to female were allowed to participate in girls' sporting events. Other practical considerations were given for those who had transitioned or were in the process of transitioning.

As the American mindset on sexuality shifted, these churches were forced to fully define and explain their views. Long-time congregants and newcomers asked specific, pointed questions. The mushy middle was no longer a viable path. Non-traditional churches, in particular, faced tension within their congregations as they sought to navigate these divisive issues.

Blow-Up In NODA

One interesting story came from Pastor Asher Smith, who planted a church in Charlotte, North Carolina in 2029. Asher graduated from college and sensed the Lord leading him and his wife to start a church in the central area of the city. They chose a neighborhood called "NODA," or "North of Davidson." This name referred to several blocks north of Davidson Street and the city's central business district. At the time, this was a historic arts and entertainment district with an eclectic combination of restaurants, bars, shops, and artists' studios. Asher and his wife, Jennifer, fit in with the abundance of twenty-somethings who called this part of the city their home. They were newly married with no children. They rented a small one-bedroom apartment in the heart of NODA. They had the freedom to spend time getting to know their neighbors and the residents of their community. They started a Bible study in their home. Eventually, they outgrew their small apartment and moved to a restaurant/bar that was closed on Sundays. On Sunday evenings, they transformed the restaurant into a small worship venue. They called their gathering *Relevant Church of NODA*.

Initially, only a handful of individuals showed up to these Sunday evening meetings. However, after six months of stagnant attendance, the church began to grow. *Exponentially*. They moved from the restaurant to an old warehouse that had been converted into an art studio, renting a portion of the building that the studio wasn't using. But then, this church grew even more. Fortunately for them, the art studio was unable to sustain their business and offered the entire building to the church. Only a year into their venture, the church had over 1000 attending each Sunday evening.

During this rapid growth phase, Asher quickly hired other staff to assist with the worship meetings and programs. While the adults gathered for worship each Sunday evening, the church offered activities for preschoolers and children. There wasn't a need for student ministry programming simply because there were no families with teenagers in the church. Virtually everyone who attended was under thirty-five years of age. Half of those who attended were singles in their twenties. Asher often commented that much of the church's growth was because their Sunday evening gatherings were the best opportunity in the week for a single person to meet a potential dating partner.

Asher was a good communicator, and those who attended enjoyed his messages. Church members often commented on how his teaching was extremely practical. Asher regularly spoke on Sunday evenings about issues those attending would face on Monday morning. Sermon titles included: *How to Manage Money; How to Deal with Difficult People; Learning How to Rest Well; Facing Your Giants.*

For two years, Relevant Church grew rapidly, and everything went extremely well.

Then, suddenly, it didn't.

The church faced an issue that caused the entire ministry to crumble. Amid such rapid growth, Asher hired a young man from within the congregation to lead the small group ministry of the church. David was a single guy, 27 years old, who worked for one of the large banks in Charlotte and was an absolute master with spreadsheets. Asher hired him to recruit and train leaders, as well as manage all the details of the small group ministry. These groups met in homes, coffee shops, and restaurants throughout the week. With David in place, Asher was then able to give his time to sermon preparation, meetings with church members, and various appointments with other individuals in the community. As well, church leaders were hoping to purchase a building, which meant he had to give hours of his time to phone calls and video conferences with real estate agents, architects, and accountants.

As a result of this busy schedule, Asher felt that he was out of the loop when it came to what was happening in the lives of church members and attendees. Moreover, he had failed to adequately download his own beliefs and DNA into David's life. As a result, Asher failed to see the coming storm.

It was a cold January morning when he received the email. It was from a church member named Danny. Asher didn't know Danny personally; however, Danny very much felt a connection with Asher. He began his email by thanking Asher for leading the church so well and for how much his sermons meant to him. Danny let him know that he had found a home at Relevant Church and thanked Asher for all his hard work.

The reason for his email was to know if Danny would be available to officiate his upcoming wedding. He and his partner, Joe, were planning to get married in May at a venue located just outside of Charlotte. He asked several other questions: *Would Asher offer premarital counseling? What fee would he charge for the ceremony? Would he and his wife be able to attend the rehearsal dinner the night before the wedding?* He then thanked Asher again for all he did at the church and closed by letting him know that he looked forward to seeing him on Sunday.

Asher sat at his desk in stunned silence. Looking back, he realized that he had not preached one sermon on marriage or sexuality in the previous two years. He did a brief series on love and relationships one February, but mainly talked about singleness and finding complete, unconditional love in Christ. Whether it was intentional or not, he simply didn't address Biblical views on sexuality.

Following is an excerpt from Asher's blog:

I immediately called our small groups director. "David," I said. "I need to meet with you right now."

He came to my office, and I read the email to him. "So, what's the problem?" David asked, sensing my discomfort but not grasping the gravity of this situation.

"David, I can't perform a same-sex wedding ceremony. It goes against my beliefs."

"It does?"

"David, are you okay with it?"

"I mean, I think so. When I worked at the bank, I knew several employees who were married to people of the same sex. It's just kinda the way it is these days. And Danny is a great guy. He leads a singles small group that has just exploded with more and more people coming every week. He's such a great leader and people are really drawn to him. He's been dating Joe for a while, and I sorta expected this was coming."

Oh, man, I thought. This was all my fault. In my excitement about the growth of our church, and knowing that I needed help, I hired David too quickly. I never asked David questions about his beliefs on marriage or sexuality. I think I assumed he believed as I did. I taught from the Bible. We used small group studies that pulled their ideas from Scripture. We were clear that we believed in the authority of the Bible. I guess we just never really addressed this specific issue.

"David, this is bad," I said. "This can be really explosive and divisive. If I say 'no' to this wedding, I might lose my church."

"Okay, then say 'yes,'" David replied.

"If I say, 'yes,' then I will lose my soul."

Sigh.

No matter what I decided, this was going to be bad for me and the rest of Relevant Church.

In the blog, Pastor Asher Smith went on to describe how he met one-on-one with Danny and explained his views on same-sex marriage. He simply couldn't officiate the ceremony, and he was sorry that his views weren't clearly explained before Danny joined the church. According to the blog, Asher was kind, gentle, and humble in his meeting with Danny; however, the conversation quickly became tense. Danny didn't like being judged and condemned for his sexuality. He marched out of the coffee shop where the two had agreed to meet, leaving Asher sitting in a booth contemplating the storm that was headed his way.

The next morning, Asher opened his computer and saw his inbox was flooded with emails. A few contained questions about the rumors swirling around the church. Some gave Asher support for his "traditional, Biblical view of marriage." But most condemned him for his narrow-minded, hurtful refusal to officiate Danny and Joe's wedding ceremony. Several emails demanded that Asher immediately apologize to both and agree to marry this wonderful couple. *Failure to do so*, these emails read, *would mean they and hundreds of others would leave the church.*

The blog was written the month after Relevant Church closed its doors and disbanded forever. The controversy was so volatile that the elders of the church believed it would do more harm than good to try to bring some sort of resolution to the situation. Those who disagreed with Pastor Asher would be better off going to another church. While those who agreed with the pastor could stay and slog through the coming weeks and months, the elders believed it wasn't worth it. NODA was a notoriously liberal-minded community. The public perception of the church had become decidedly negative. The elders believed it would be impossible to continue ministry in that community.

Relevant Church wasn't alone. Hundreds of other churches experienced a similar fate. Some attempted to weather the controversy, only to find their numbers dwindle to the point that the ministry became unsustainable.

The culture's changing views on sexuality forced this brand of churches to clearly articulate what had previously been left unsaid or ambiguous. In contrast to the churches mentioned in the previous chapter, it wasn't a shift from traditional, orthodox views that caused these churches to decline. Rather, it was the absence of a well-defined theology that led to their demise. Throughout the 2030s, these previously booming churches saw a rapid decline in attendance, with many hosting their final worship services and closing their doors forever.

As the changing cultural views on marriage and sexuality caused churches to fall out of favor with society, an internal problem did even further damage to the reputation of Christianity in America. This particular issue affected Protestant, Catholic, and nondenominational churches alike. Both conservative and liberal churches had to deal with this matter. While the perception of churches in America was already on the decline, multiple reports of actions by pastors and religious leaders contributed greatly to the growing negative opinion of churches held by the majority in our nation.

I cover this sixth thread of the death shroud in the next chapter.

CHAPTER 6

Sullied by Scandals

How Immoral Behavior Eroded Public Trust

I n his article, *The Three Worlds of Evangelicalism*, written in February of 2022, Aaron Renn made a case for three distinct periods of the American church. He refers to these blocks of time as "worlds."

- **Positive World** (Pre-1994): Society at large retains a mostly positive view of Christianity. Renn argued that, in this stage, the American culture looked at church membership and attendance through a generally favorable lens.
- **Neutral World** (1994–2014): Society takes a neutral stance toward Christianity. According to Renn, culture at large neither condemned nor praised church attendance in this stage.
- **Negative World** (2014–Present): Society came to have a negative view of Christianity. In 2022, Renn argued that "being known as a Christian is a social negative, particularly in the elite domains of society."[17]

Although one may quibble over the exact dates Renn assigned to each stage, this researcher believes they accurately identified the shifting attitudes of the American culture toward the Christian church. Renn argued that the reason behind these transitions in the culture's view of Christians was primarily due to society's change in morals. When the church (primarily conservative, evangelical churches) didn't adjust with the culture, Christianity fell out of favor in the United States.

However, this cannot be the only reason for the change in how Americans viewed the Christian church. Conservative churches weren't the only ones falling out of favor with the general population. Across the theological spectrum, churches were in a steep decline. While Renn's timeline was accurate, other factors were behind this shift. A primary contributor to this change in perspective was the numerous scandals associated with churches and church leaders. The flood of news stories in the first few decades of this century served as a significant component of the transition in public perception.

Admittedly, there were Christian leaders who "fell from grace" during the so-called positive world. A few well-known television evangelists with large viewing audiences had very dramatic, very public scandals. However, the actions of these nationally known figures didn't seem to influence the opinions of most Americans regarding Christianity or professional clergy. Throughout most of the 1990s, the public perception of Christian pastors and priests remained largely positive. But this would not last. The church in America would soon face a public relations nightmare.

The Fall of Church Professionals

Shortly after the turn of the millennium, reports of immoral and abusive behavior began surfacing regularly. Specifically, there were countless revelations regarding offenses within the two largest denominations in the United States: The Roman Catholic Church and the Southern Baptist Convention. According to numerous reports, both religious groups made the mistake of not effectively and efficiently dealing with the abuse taking place within their churches. Allegations of priests, pastors, and church volunteers sexually abusing children, teenagers, and young adults became public, launching outcries of criticism against church leaders who had failed to set up systems of accountability and, more shockingly, ignored or minimized reports of abuse.

In 2022, the Roman Catholic Diocese of Rochester, New York—after decades of abuse claims against the church—reached a court settlement in which the church agreed to pay $55 million to victims of abuse. In a letter sent to parishioners following the report of this settlement, Bishop Salvatore Matano wrote the following:

The history of sexual abuse of children in our Church has caused tremendous pain, hardship, alienation, and understandable anger. It seriously has impacted survivors, their families, our priests, and others in diocesan ministries who had no part in these egregious acts.... This chapter in the life of our Church has also impacted everyone who has felt their own faith shaken by those who violated a sacred trust to protect the vulnerable and live according to the teachings of Jesus Christ.[18]

In 2019, the *Houston Chronicle* published an extensive report detailing the abuse of pastors and church volunteers within the Southern Baptist Convention.[19] The "bombshell" three-part series was entitled: "*Abuse of Faith: 20 years, 700 victims: Southern Baptist sexual abuse spreads as leaders resist reform.*" The 400-page report shared numerous victims' accounts and stories of reporting abusers to church and denominational leaders, only to see little or no response and no further investigation. The article also examined the lack of child-protection policies in many churches and showed how predators were easily able to obtain access to their victims.

Throughout the early part of this century, countless other accounts of sexual abuse by clergy flooded news websites. No Christian denomination was exempt. Churches in every region of the country, in every socio-economic class, and in virtually every theological stream had to deal with allegations of misconduct. This was more than a few isolated cases; rather, churches in this period saw an *epidemic* of misconduct within their ranks.

Moreover, numerous allegations were made in the early 2000s against quite a few megachurch, high-profile pastors. Seemingly year after year, there were reports of these very public figures resigning from their churches due to some sort of moral failure. In many cases, these individuals had served as the founding pastor of their church. Yet, their actions forced them to walk away from the ministry they had birthed.

In the opinion of many Christians, the greatest scandal of the 2020s centered around author and speaker Ravi Zacharias, a popular figure in evangelical Christian circles. After his death in 2020, the ministry organization he founded released a twelve-page report detailing stories of sexual assault perpetrated by Zacharias against numerous women.[20] Christian leaders throughout the country expressed their shock and dismay over these revelations.

These accounts of high-profile pastors "falling from grace" mirrored what was happening throughout the American church. Scandals occurred in small congregations, mid-sized churches, and megachurches across the nation. The abuse and misconduct happened in churches from every major Christian denomination and style—contemporary, traditional, conservative, liberal, and non-denominational. No group or "tribe" managed to remain unscathed.

While these accounts surprised and discouraged Christians, they only added to the growing cynicism felt by those outside of the church. The reputations of Christians and churches were sullied. These events served as a major catalyst in pushing the church into the negative world.

The following archived blog from 2025 illustrates the effect of these scandals and the contribution they made to the decline of the American church:

I absolutely loved our neighborhood church in Tulsa. They had a wonderful music program, a terrific ministry for my kids, and the pastor's sermons were so engaging and insightful. In almost every conversation with my friends, I would talk about my church. Several of my neighbors didn't go to church anywhere. I would see them while walking my dog, and I would always make it a point to invite them to come to our church. I told them I would be happy to meet them and sit with them. One family in our neighborhood did. The husband and wife both became followers of Christ. They and their young children came nearly every Sunday. Other neighbors heard about this, and they asked me questions. They seemed intrigued and open to visiting.

Then, the bomb dropped. Our pastor announced that he was resigning. And that he and his wife were divorcing. Apparently, he'd had an affair with a lady in our church. I think she was the wife of a deacon. It was bad and bloody. Lots of rumors circulated throughout the congregation.

Worse, though, was the family who came the year before quit going to church. So did about a third of everyone else in the church. And none of my neighbors seemed interested or open to coming after they heard about the scandal.

After a while, our family left that church and went to one several miles farther away from our home. We liked the church, but it became much harder to convince neighbors to check it out. Distance always became the go-to excuse. So, we just quit inviting.

Countless other blogs and posts referenced similar stories. The church of this period was scandal-laden. The reputation of the church in America simply was not what it had been. The culture viewed Christians and Christian leaders in a decidedly negative light.

Searching For an Explanation

What caused this phenomenon to happen in the earlier part of this century? Some argued that it was always an issue, but it wasn't widely reported in previous decades. Victims felt ashamed and hesitant to come forth with allegations, wondering if they would be believed by those in authority. Only after a brave few were willing to speak did others reveal their own accounts of abuse. These pioneers paved the way for countless victims to come forward.

While there may be some truth in this theory, the sheer volume of abuse allegations from 2000 to 2030 seems to indicate more to the story than just victims finally feeling the freedom to speak about their situations. A later study revealed that the rise in sexual abuse correlated with two significant changes in our culture.

First, it was no coincidence that these reports of sexual misconduct corresponded with universal access to the internet and the pornographic sites contained within its depths. Pastors and church leaders, throughout most of the 1900s, didn't have pornographic materials readily available to them through electronic means. Going to a retail establishment or attempting to purchase materials by calling a phone number and giving one's credit card information was far too risky. A spouse or church member might easily discover the so-called nefarious activities of this pastor.

But, around the turn of the century, the internet gave nearly unfettered access to pornography and the ability to view these websites inconspicuously. Simply put, individuals, including pastors, were able to engage in this activity secretly and privately. According to a 2016 study, most pastors (57 percent) and youth pastors (64 percent) admitted they struggled with porn at some point in their lives.[21]

This certainly wasn't restricted to professional clergy. So-called sexual misconduct was rampant across the culture. Teachers in schools were arrested and convicted for abuse. In 2022 alone, nearly 350 educators in our nation were arrested for sex crimes, almost all of which were perpetrated against students.[22] Other institutions and organizations within our nation also saw a rise in crimes against minors. The Boy Scouts of America, for example, dealt with numerous scandals and lawsuits. A 2020 documentary noted that 82,000 individuals had come forward with claims of abuse against this organization's leaders.[23]

Thus, the abuse was not just a problem within the church. It was a widespread phenomenon resulting from open access to what was once very restricted photos and videos. As the American culture became highly sexualized in the early part of this century, reports of unwanted and inappropriate sexual advances increased dramatically. To blame the precipitous rise in abuse solely on this new access to online "pornography" would be an overstatement. To point to this as the primary reason for the increase would not.

New Behavior with Old-Fashioned Morals

The second reason for the vast number of scandals, ironically, is that the culture's and church's views on sexual activity remained vastly outdated. In the first few decades of the twenty-first century, many of the headlines about church leaders related to extramarital affairs. Daniel Hampton, for example, served as the pastor of New

City Church in Nevada. Moreover, he was elected President of the American Council of Evangelical Churches in 2030.

However, in 2034, he was dismissed from both the church and his position with ACEC due to a same-sex, extramarital affair. In his resignation letter, Hampton wrote:

> The fact is, I am guilty of gross sexual immorality. I have failed my family, my church family, and the Lord. I take entire responsibility for the situation I have created.

By the ethical standards of our day, the actions of Hampton certainly wouldn't be considered "gross immorality." Fulfilling one's sexual desires is now considered as natural as breathing. Except for the very few narrow-minded Christians remaining in the shadows of our nation, no one would expect a leader of any organization to resign over a normal human function. The fact that Hampton referred to his actions as a failure clearly shows how far we have advanced in our understanding of human ethics.

Moreover, many of the so-called scandals involved pastors who had sexual relationships with minors. However, the *Sexual Choice Act* passed by Congress in 2045 now allows these relationships as long as no physical harm is imposed upon the minor participant. Although it took several decades, the legislative and judicial systems finally recognized the validity of various human proclivities and the necessity of satisfying these urges. No longer is the possession and distribution of any pornographic material a crime, regardless of the age of the subject being filmed or photographed. No longer is it a crime to engage in a consensual sexual relationship, regardless of the age of either party. Our nation has now embraced the oft-repeated motto of those who initially promoted this legislation: *Age is just a number!* SCA has—according to most in our society—freed us from the oppressive restraints of former generations.

Additionally, this law has dramatically reduced the number of crimes against minors. While there were 350 educators in 2022 arrested for sex crimes, charges were filed against only two individuals in 2052. Most believe these new laws have allowed our police and courts to focus their resources on solving actual crimes rather than investigating the actions of two people who are in love fulfilling their natural desires.

As well, the courts are no longer flooded with frivolous lawsuits against individuals for using positions of power to coerce others into unwanted sexual situations. Again, the culture's enlightened view of this normal human activity has allowed a "live and let live" mentality to permeate our society. Love is love, and the idea of judging and condemning others for the way they fulfill their desires for love and sex is minimally present in America today.

Moreover, the creation of a "genderless" society, aided by the passing of such bills as the LGBTQ+ Protect Act, has eliminated unnecessary, outdated slogans such as the *#MeToo* bandwagon of the 20s. Without the unfounded notions regarding "male aggressiveness," accusations of abuse are rarely reported unless there is actual proof of physical trauma brought about from the actions of another individual or individuals.

However, in the early part of this century, these actions perpetrated by church leaders were considered immoral by the culture at large and in violation of Christians' own stated standards of belief. The numerous news reports regarding these sexual scandals caused great damage to the public perception of the church. The culture increasingly viewed the American church in a decidedly negative light.

But Wait, There's More

The rise in sexual scandals was undoubtedly detrimental to the reputation of the Christian church in America. However, there were also other, non-sexual scandals. Multiple accounts of pastors abusing power, stealing from churches, or using their positions of authority to demean subordinates were reported with increasing frequency.

One such account came to light in an extremely popular podcast entitled *The Birth and Death of Athens Church*. This 20-episode podcast told the story of a former megachurch located in Minneapolis, Minnesota. The editors described in great detail the explosive growth of the church in the years after it began in 2025 and the internal implosion which caused the church to close its doors in 2034. Several former church members accused the founding pastor, Peter Durham, of lying, intimidation, and a general abuse of power. The podcast featured segments of sermons delivered by Pastor Durham and interviews of individuals who were deeply involved in the church. The revelation of this popular, generally well-regarded pastor allegedly displaying manipulative behavior and mistreating underlings shocked many, both inside and outside the church. This disclosure fed the already growing cynicism toward Christian churches possessed by growing numbers within the American population.

Around this same time, there were countless other headlines regarding the varied misconduct of pastors and other church leaders. The culture's negative view of the Christian church was certainly exacerbated by these regular, prolific accounts of behavior inconsistent with the beliefs and teachings held by Christians. Following are just a few of the more prominent headlines from this period:

- Arizona Pastor Pleads Guilty to Wire Fraud after Purchasing $100,000 BMW with Fraudulent Pandemic Disaster Loan
- Pastor among 79 Arrested in Virginia Drug Raid
- New York Pastor Charged with Bilking Federal Program to Feed Needy Kids, Spending $130,000 on Luxury Vacations
- California Pastor Released After Serving Sentence for Theft from Elderly Couple
- Chicago Church Employee Sentenced After Stealing $350,000 to Fund Gambling Trips: "Fueled by pure greed"

From 2010-2035, hundreds of headlines appeared each year regarding misdeeds within churches. However, these stories appeared far less frequently in the decades following 2035 for the following reason: the number of church closings in those years significantly reduced the number of pastors and church leaders. There were fewer and fewer individuals in churches to commit crimes and abuses.

The scandals in the first few decades of the 21st century did great damage to the reputation of the church. Pastors were, in prior years, among the most respected members of society. However, the inundation of public scandals severely eroded this trust. A 2031 survey asked 1000 Americans to rank 40 professions in light of the question: "Who do you consider to be the most trustworthy?" "Members of the Clergy" placed 34th, just ahead of "Hedge Fund Managers" and "Congressional Representatives," respectively. Simply put, pastors and priests became suspect members of society in the eyes of most Americans, which only served to accelerate the now rapid deterioration of the church in America.

Like a patient in the ICU fighting for their life, many churches were just one crisis away from death.

That crisis hit in early 2020.

CHAPTER 7

The COVID-19 Pandemic of 2020

Government Mandates against Worship Gatherings

The COVID-19 (acronym for Coronavirus Disease) pandemic of 2019 and 2020 dealt a major blow to the church in America. In the fall of 2019, reports began circulating about an unusual virus spreading from China—where it reportedly originated—to other countries in Asia and into Eastern and Western Europe. In January 2020, this same virus hit the shores of America, landing on the West Coast, and eventually making its way across the continental United States.

In March 2020, most state governors declared a state of emergency and either requested or required the cessation of all public gatherings, including church worship services. Initially, governmental authorities claimed that a two-week quarantine would be sufficient to halt the rapidly spreading virus. Seemingly overnight, Americans shifted their everyday routines. Schools announced that they were closing their doors, ostensibly, for a couple of weeks. Sports practices and games were delayed, then later postponed indefinitely or canceled altogether. Businesses, restaurants, and entertainment venues closed their doors. Individuals who were able to work from home did. Others stayed home and became effectively unemployed, even though their employers never officially terminated these employees.

The mandates against all public gatherings meant that thousands of churches did not meet for weeks, months, or, in some cases, the next year or two. Churches attempted to keep their members engaged through various online resources. They streamed their worship services each week. These videos most often featured a pastor preaching in an empty sanctuary. In many cases, they contained worship music performed by a band or orchestra. Some churches held worship gatherings in out-door venues, requiring participants to place at least six feet of distance between themselves and non-family members. When churches regathered inside buildings, they severely limited the number who could attend. Worshippers were required to "socially distance" themselves from one another. There were no hugs, handshakes, or close conversations.

Everything had changed.

It was a strange time in our nation's history; however, for churches, the COVID pandemic and the resulting quarantine became the moment in time that the Christian church in America took a notable turn for the worse. Specifically, there were four results of this pandemic on the church in America.

Impetus to the Inevitable

First, the COVID pandemic had a particularly detrimental effect on those churches who were already in decline. The quarantine caused an acceleration of their downward spiral. In 2026, approximately six years after the start of the pandemic, *The Hatcher Group* commissioned an extensive survey of 50,000 Protestant churches in the United States. This research project revealed, in part, the following:

> For many churches, the COVID pandemic was like a fast-forward button on a video documenting the lifespan of the church. For example, an analysis of a church pre-COVID might have determined that the church—assuming no changes to its current trajectory—had another ten years before this congregation would be forced to close its doors and disband. COVID cut most of those estimates in half so that this example church had only five years of life left.
>
> Interestingly, our research indicated that in many cases, this acceleration was delayed due to the incredible amount of liquidity pumped into the economy by the federal government. As a result, numbers of churches fared much better financially than what would've been the case in a typical economy. They managed to continue paying staff salaries and funding ministries even though their attendance numbers were in precipitous decline. However, once the money was gone and the worship gatherings saw only sparse attendance, difficult decisions had to be made.

Over the last five years, many churches were forced to hold final worship services and close their doors forever.

Only 2 percent of Protestant churches who were in decline before the pandemic managed to reverse this trend after COVID. For the remaining 98 percent, the downward spiral increased rapidly. The researchers with The Hatcher Group estimated that, as of June 2026, nearly 75,000 churches died prematurely—meaning, these churches had disbanded sometime between the start of the pandemic and the date the research project was commissioned, and their death was directly related to the impact of COVID on the ministry of the church.

Further research revealed the primary cause of the rapid decline and death of these churches was due to a new post-COVID reality. Simply put, "Cultural Christians" quit going to church. For many years, these individuals attended church out of a sense of expectation, obligation, or simple habit. They had no personal commitment to their faith; rather, they enjoyed the fellowship, the tradition, the moral lessons, or other periphery aspects of the worship and ministry of the church. When churches quit meeting during the quarantine for weeks or months, these cultural Christians either found these needs met through other means or decided these church benefits weren't critical to their happiness and joy as human beings. The author of the Hatcher article asserted that almost one-third of churchgoers fell into this category, thus leaving a significant gap between pre-COVID and post-COVID attendance for most churches.

While many pastors bemoaned the lower attendance numbers, the difficulties most churches faced weren't due to COVID;

rather, they were directly related to the numbers of non-Christians who attended their churches for all of the years before the pandemic. COVID simply revealed the reality of non-Christian membership. Had the churches addressed their cultural Christianity problem prior to 2020, the effects of the quarantine would've been less severe.

The Great Reset

A second issue for many churches was the "reset" offered by the cessation of worship and other meetings during the spring and summer of 2020. Researchers estimated that, generally, a third of church members remained with their church, a third went to other churches, and a third quit going altogether. According to the research identified earlier, the last third were primarily cultural Christians who ceased attending any worship gatherings.

However, a third of church members returned to church gatherings after the end of the quarantine, just not at the church they formerly attended. The pandemic offered these individuals an escape hatch. Many Christians had been considering, for some time, making a change. They were dissatisfied with their church but hadn't found the opportunity to gracefully exit and begin looking for another church home. COVID offered that opportunity. When churches discontinued their worship meetings and other ministry gatherings, these dissatisfied members seized the opportunity for change.

Overall, this "reset" moment in the history of American Christianity had a detrimental effect on smaller, "family-style" churches. These churches typically had fewer than fifty attendees on a Sunday but managed to cultivate an intimate, friendly atmosphere with strong relational bonds. However, the quality and quantity of ministry offerings were lacking. Some of these churches, for example, had only one child in the children's ministry or virtually nothing to offer teenagers. When the quarantine ended, many of these churches discovered that only the most loyal core members returned, and families with children at home gravitated toward churches with more ministry offerings.

This reality contributed to the growth of some mid-size and larger churches. In the six years following the COVID pandemic, roughly 15 percent of Protestant churches experienced some measure of growth in their overall attendance. Effectively, the number of churches closing their doors each year outpaced the decline in overall church attendance. While weekly worship attendance among Protestant churches declined by 35 percent during this period, the number of actual churches declined by 50 percent. Simply put, churches with more ministry offerings grew, while churches with fewer programs declined and died.

Decision Fatigue

Third, numerous churches were weakened because their pastors became discouraged and weary during the pandemic. For leaders of most businesses and organizations, there were multiple difficulties navigating the ever-changing and often conflicting recommendations of national, state, and local officials. However, for churches, the challenges were especially complex. Multiple blogs posted in the aftermath of COVID revealed how overwhelmed pastors felt during this period of their ministry. A post by one anonymous pastor stated the following:

> I put together a committee of members to assist our church in making decisions on the myriad of issues we faced. Except, the members of the committee couldn't seem to agree on the next best steps. For example, should we require masks to be worn during worship? One committee member stated, emphatically, that we should absolutely require everyone to wear a mask during the entire time they are in the building. She even pulled up information from the CDC on her iPad and cited chapter and verse on why we should require masks to be worn.
>
> Another committee member, who is a doctor of internal medicine, laughed and said, "Unless they are all N95 masks, they are pretty much useless. Why are we requiring masks if they don't really make a difference?"

Masks, it seems, were not the only controversial issue. Individuals offered vastly different answers to virtually every question asked. Should the church require reservations for worship attendance? Should someone take their temperature when they enter the building? What is the best method to enforce social distancing? When should programming for preschoolers, children, and students resume? Should three-year-olds be required to wear masks? Can this even possibly be managed? What if someone informs the church that they attended worship and later tested positive for COVID? Does the church have an obligation to notify everyone in the church?

Once the COVID vaccine became available, there were more questions and even more divisions. Church members disagreed vehemently over what the proper approach should be in protecting those who attended worship. Should the vaccine be required to gain admittance into the building? Is verbal verification enough, or should individuals be asked to show a vaccination card? What if they had COVID and recovered? Is that as effective as the vaccine?

No question had a simple answer. Committees met and discussed and disagreed and then discussed some more. In the case of the pastor mentioned above, the committee ultimately looked to him to make the final decision. Since he would be faced with the most questions, they wanted to give him the freedom to decide the next best steps for the church.

Great. That meant I had to make decisions that had no easy answer and were guaranteed to make someone unhappy. If I said, "We need to wear masks," half the people thought I was kowtowing to the Democrats who just wanted to control everything. If I said, "Let's resume Sunday School for preschoolers and children," I was endangering lives and single-handedly killing countless people in our church and community. No matter what decision was made, some group was unhappy, and I was the target of their ire.

A member called me one morning and said, "Pastor, I hope you go ahead and get the vaccine as soon as it's available, and then tell everyone in the church to follow your example. People look up to you and you will help save lives if you do that." Not fifteen minutes later, a man called me and said, "Pastor, I sure hope you're not planning on getting the COVID vaccine. I just read a report that these shots are really bad for your heart. Plus, as a man of God, I think you should just trust in the Lord's plan. If you get COVID, I'm sure that there is a reason."

Good grief. I'm just so tired.

This anonymous pastor wasn't the only one who felt exhausted and overwhelmed by all that he faced during the COVID pandemic. Numerous articles from the years immediately following this period cited studies highlighting the mental and emotional exhaustion of pastors.

This condition of so many pastors had three effects on churches. First, many pastors retired prematurely. Those who were financially able to do so retired a year or two earlier than they'd planned before the pandemic began. For these pastors, the COVID pandemic opened the door for an earlier-than-expected exit from the ministry.

Another group of pastors resigned and found jobs outside of the church. The average rate of pastor attrition before the pandemic was 1 percent annually.[24] So, 1 in every 100 pastors left the ministry before their retirement. From 2022-2027, this statistic grew to an average of 3 percent attrition each year. Clearly, the issues faced during the pandemic caused many pastors to merely give up and find alternative forms of employment.

The third group of ministers stayed and continued to pastor their churches; however, they no longer had the same zeal and desire to lead. They continued to perform the duties required of them, but they ceased to inspire others or approach their jobs with the same passion they possessed prior to the pandemic. In many ways, they "quiet quit," a form of resignation in which the individual continues to show up to a job and go through the motions of work while only doing the minimally required tasks.

Churches naturally suffered and declined as a result of losing their pastors to retirement, resignation, or passivity. Without leaders, these churches didn't have the same effectiveness in their ministries. The decade after the COVID pandemic was a difficult chapter in the life of the American church.

Separation of Church and State?

The fourth issue created by the pandemic was the question of the state's right to impose mandatory restrictions on churches. When COVID began spreading rapidly throughout the United States in February and March of 2020, state and local governments immediately prohibited public gatherings.

In most cases, organizations, sports teams, and public venues voluntarily followed these mandates. The unknowns of this novel virus caused tremendous fear among the American population. During the early stages of the pandemic, most individuals in our nation isolated themselves and had little interest in attending any large gatherings.

Virtually all churches initially complied with these restrictions. Again, the unknowns and flood of ever-changing information caused our entire nation to push the pause button on normal activities, including the attendance of worship gatherings.

However, several weeks into the pandemic and resulting quarantine, numerous churches decided to defy these government mandates and resume in-person worship gatherings. Grace Community Church in Los Angeles, California, was the most notable example of a congregation gathering in violation of government mandates. The pastor of this church, John MacArthur, announced that his church would hold worship services in July 2020 in violation of public health orders banning indoor gatherings for religious meetings. According to an article from *Christianity Today* in 2021:

> Attorneys representing MacArthur filed a suit in August 2020 against California Gov. Gavin Newsom and other state, city, and county officials, saying the state's restrictions on large group meetings and singing restricted its religious freedom. County officials then sued the church to require it to comply with COVID-19 protocols—including barring large group indoor worship and requiring social distancing at outdoor worship.[25]

The battle between the church and government officials made its way through the legal system in the case of *Harvest Rock Church, et al. v. Newsom.* In February 2021, the attorneys for each side argued this case before the United States Supreme Court. The court ruled in favor of the churches, although it allowed government officials to cap indoor gatherings at 25 percent of capacity.[26]

In the years following the pandemic, questions arose over the state's legal authority over church affairs. Did local and state governments possess the right to demand the cessation of worship gatherings in churches? Was this only applicable during a pandemic, or do government officials have the right to restrict or ban worship gatherings in other cases?

In 2048, in the case of *Calvary Church v. Anderson*, the Supreme Court settled this lingering question. The state of California enacted a law disallowing the gathering of any religious group unless every member of the church signed a state-drafted "tolerance pledge" affirming and recognizing the "beliefs and practices of the multicultural, nonuniform population of California as valid for a healthy, diverse society." The aim of this tolerance pledge was to forbid pastors and ministers in these churches from teaching absolute truths regarding religious beliefs or moral practices. The state successfully argued that allowing this language in public settings would create a level of intolerance that endangered public health. Soon after the Supreme Court ruled in favor of California, other states quickly enacted similar laws.

Churches asserted their First Amendment rights, both in freedom of speech and, more specifically, the constitution's protection against Congress making any law "respecting an establishment of religion or prohibiting the free exercise thereof."[27] The Supreme Court, however, ruled that these restrictions only applied to the Federal Government and not to the states. Ultimately, church members who refused to sign these pledges were forced to meet secretly in homes rather than gather in public venues.

The 2020s and 30s were challenging decades for the church in America. When the calendar turned to 2040, the church was still alive, but her heartbeat was faint and her breathing shallow. While committed churchgoers panicked at the situation, most

Americans didn't even notice or care about the impending death of the church. When additional laws restricting the speech allowed in churches were passed, the outcry of Christians generated little attention. Major headlines featured only the most notable legislation or Supreme Court decisions. By the end of the 2040s, the church's rights were quickly diminishing. The church was on life-support, and most Americans were more than happy to let it die.

CHAPTER 8

DON'T SAY NO GAY

When Christian Beliefs Became Hate Speech

In December 2022, hundreds of citizens in Louden County, Virginia, gathered for a local school board meeting. There, a concerned parent addressed the district's transgender policy and the report of a biological male student wearing a skirt, entering a female restroom, and assaulting two female students. In criticizing the policy, the parent paraphrased a passage from the Bible:

> "If any man or woman causes one of these little ones to stumble, it would be better for [them] if a millstone to be put around [their] neck and thrown into the lake."[28]

In response to this parent's speech, a community organizer drafted a petition calling on the school board to ban hate speech at public meetings. This individual specifically referenced as "hate speech" the Bible passage quoted at this earlier meeting. The petition received hundreds of signatures, and in December 2023, the school board voted unanimously to "disallow any reference to a religious holy book at any public meeting, including but not limited to the Bible, Koran, or Bhagavad Gita."[29] At the time, the enforcement of this policy was limited to simply cutting off the microphone of any speaker who used religious language. In the coming years, however, federal, state, and local governments introduced stronger punishments for those who violated such hate speech laws.

In November 2022, the United States Senate voted on and passed the "Respect for Marriage Act." President Joe Biden signed this bill into legislation, protecting same-sex marriage if the United States Supreme Court ever overturned the *Obergefell* decision.[30] That President Biden, a Democrat, signed this bill wasn't surprising to anyone. However, the fact that this was bipartisan legislation passed with the support of twelve Republican Senators demonstrated the national change in attitude toward same-sex marriages. Noted by one reporter:

> In a sign of how much support has grown in recent years for same-sex marriage, the bill found backing from GOP senators including those in deeply red states...Utah Sen. Mitt Romney, meanwhile, said..., "While I believe in traditional marriage, Obergefell is and has been the law of the land upon which LGBTQ individuals have relied."[31]

Romney was not only a Republican senator from Utah, but he was also the 2012 Republican candidate for President of the United States. His support for this bill was evidence of the national mindset shift on this issue.

In opposition to the *Respect for Marriage Act* was Republican senator James Lankford of Oklahoma. Lankford argued that this bill would not just serve as a shield for same-sex marriage but would become a sword used to punish any groups opposed to homosexual marriage:

[They] are no longer saying, "We demand recognition" of same-sex marriage. Now they're saying, "We're going to crush anyone that opposes our belief in gay marriage."[32]

Senator Lankford's statement turned out to be quite prescient. In 2036, the California state legislature debated the newly introduced *Incitement to Hatred Bill,* one which sought to criminalize any speech opposing same-sex relationships or gender transitions. In what became a highly publicized speech before this body, Senator John Hampton stated:

Yes, you have rights, but they are restricted for the common good. Just as one cannot yell, "Fire!" in a crowded theater, one cannot speak in such a manner to make others feel unsafe, insecure, and cause them such deep discomfort that they cannot live in peace. I believe that it is our job as legislators to restrict those freedoms for the benefit of our society as a whole.

In 2037, this bill was passed and signed into law. Soon after, other states passed laws prohibiting and criminalizing any written or verbal language that condemned either sexual preferences or gender identity claims. As these new laws gained traction in the United States, pressure increased for federal, uniform legislation to deal with "hate speech" commonly espoused by the few Christians remaining in our nation.

After years of debate, President Inman, in her 2045 inaugural address to the nation, summarized well the course America would take regarding the intersection of religion and freedom from discrimination:

It has been vehemently and vigorously argued that the Constitution guarantees our citizens the freedom to exercise their religion. I agree with this statement; however, it doesn't guarantee anyone to practice their religion at the expense of other Americans. For far too long, Christians have used the First Amendment both as a shield and a sword. They have drawn this freedom from their scabbards and used it to cut those in the LGBTQ+ communities with their primitive beliefs regarding so-called sexual "virtues." Then, when they have been confronted regarding their hateful words, they've attempted to use the First Amendment as a shield, cowardly crouching behind it as they scream and cry about their constitutional rights.

Fellow citizens, I ask this: what about the rights of others to live as accepted people in our society? What about the rights of your LGBTQ+ neighbors and friends to be free from social media posts claiming their lifestyle is less moral than anyone else's?

For the last three decades, Christians have claimed the right to deny services to LGBTQ+ individuals. They have refused to bake cakes or print invitations for their union ceremonies. They've declined requests to serve as photographers or videographers at polygamous weddings. They've discriminated in numerous ways and then attempted to justify their actions by claiming religious freedom.

Today, my administration is putting these bigoted individuals on notice. I say to them, "No more. *No. More.*"

President Inman then urged Congress to pass and send her a bill criminalizing any public language condemning or belittling those in the LGBTQ+ community. She asked for heavy fines to be imposed upon those possessing written or verbal attacks of same-sex, multi-partner, adult-child, or open relationships. The President even called for the removal of Bibles from public spaces, including hotel rooms. Citing these outdated religious morals as "the last vestige of discrimination in our nation," she implored all Americans to join her in making "our society a place where there is "truly liberty and justice for all."

The President's inaugural address was well received by most Americans. President Inman was the first member of the LGBTQ+ community to be elected President and—according to many Presidential historians—she was the most telegenic individual to ever occupy the Oval Office. David Barnhouse, the author of Inman's biography, *The Pride of POTUS,* wrote:

The camera loved her even more than it loved Ronald Reagan. And her team knew this. They hired the best social media experts in the country to post clip after clip of her speeches. When she debated her opponents—both in the primaries and in the general election—none stood a chance. She was a master of the witty comeback and the perfectly timed joke. Her beautiful smile, affable manner, and brilliant mind made her the perfect politician.

During her campaign, Inman promised to "fully and unashamedly affirm those in the LGBTQ+ community and work tirelessly for their full acceptance as Americans." Throughout her candidacy, she made compelling, reasonable arguments for why more legislation was needed to end discrimination against these individuals. Voters not only liked her personally, but they also agreed with her ideas. In virtually every poll, Americans empathized with Inman and agreed that the fight to end discrimination was not finished.

On June 18, 2046, Congress passed the *LGBTQ+ Protection Act* (LPA), or what became dubbed by the media as the *"Don't Say No Gay Law."* This legislation defined as "hate speech" all non-affirming language regarding same-sex and multi-partner relationships. Using its powers granted under the interstate commerce clause of the Constitution, the Federal Government enforced this ban on all forms of media accessible across the various states. This legislation criminalized any speech elevating the marriage of a man and a woman as superior to other marriage or partnered relationships. These regulatory powers applied to television, radio, and the internet. Technically, it also applied to any media in print form mailed across a state line; however, the strict regulation on printed media and the elimination of the United States Post Office in 2049 made irrelevant this section of the legislation.

The LPA also allocated over $800 billion in new annual funding to the Federal Transmissions Commission. The FTC became the enforcing arm of the government, hiring thousands of agents to both proactively find violators and respond to complaints from citizens.

All television and radio programs were forced to carefully monitor their language. A talk-show commentator who spoke negatively regarding any individual in the LGBTQ+ community was immediately canceled. Hefty fines were levied on the parent company of the radio station. Television programs and Hollywood movies faced the same regulations, although most were in favor of and readily followed these new laws.

Many churches, however, found themselves immediately in the crosshairs of the FTC. Churches with verbiage on their websites regarding a belief in traditional marriage were placed on notice. The language would have to be changed or removed from the website, or the FTC would use its new powers to remove the entire website from the internet.

Moreover, churches were forced to make decisions regarding the live streaming of their worship services. Software programs were able to identify any songs or spoken words that violated the LPA. A Sunday morning broadcast would many times be followed by a Monday morning phone call or, in some cases, FTC agents appearing at the doors of church offices. Churches were allowed to keep their websites in operation if they immediately paid the fine and posted a written apology for the offensive language. The initial legislation imposed $2,000 for the first offense and $5,000 for the second and third offenses. Media licenses were suspended on the fourth offense. In 2054, the LPA was amended to increase the fine to $5,000 for the first offense with immediate suspension for subsequent violations.

As previously noted, Christian churches in America divided over the issue of same-sex attraction. Most mainline Protestant denominations took the stance of affirming gay and lesbian marriages as morally acceptable relationships. Most conservative Protestant and Roman Catholic churches believed and taught the traditional Christian view of marriage: "a union between one man and one woman."

In the late 40s and early 50s, the FTC effectively ignored those churches that adopted a favorable view toward same-sex marriage. These congregations were allowed to continue their operations without interference from the government. It wasn't until the late 2050s that these churches began receiving phone calls and visits from FTC agents.

The more conservative churches, though, were forced to move out of the public eye. Websites either became nondescript or were completely removed from the internet. Live streams ceased. Visitors to worship gatherings immediately became suspect. Any individual in a congregation could secretly video the sermon and then upload that video to a social media page with information about the church's location. The FTC would immediately jump into action.

Larger, conservative congregations were unable to continue their normal operations. By 2050, those churches virtually disappeared from the American landscape. These congregations moved to underground networks, often meeting in church members' homes. Campuses were sold, and the money from the sale was used to help fund the salaries of the additional pastors required to manage the decentralized network of individuals associated with the church.

A notable example of this legislation's power is seen in what happened to Western Shore Church in Vancouver, Washington. In 2025, this church averaged 5,000 to 6,000 attendees on a weekend. They held multiple worship gatherings at six different locations in Vancouver and neighboring Portland, Oregon. Between 2025 and 2030, the congregation nearly doubled, averaging almost 10,000 on a weekend. A blog maintained by a church member, David Johnson, detailed the explosive growth during that period. In a blog entry dated November 24, 2029, Mr. Johnson wrote the following:

On this Thanksgiving weekend, I cannot help but reflect on all that has happened at Western Shore. It's been amazing to watch how the Lord has blessed our church in immeasurable ways. Five years ago, something began that has been hard for anyone to really explain. I read our pastor's article in the newsletter this week. This past Sunday, our worship attendance was over 11,000, almost double the attendance of this same weekend five years ago. I'm thankful not only that the Lord has saved me but allowed me to be a part of this incredible church.

When Western Shore exploded in growth, the church caught the attention of the Vancouver populace. The pastors and leadership suddenly found themselves being scrutinized by politicians and the media. The ire of their surrounding community intensified when, in 2031, Pastor Eric Howell preached a series on marriage. In one Sunday morning sermon, Howell unapologetically stated that a sexual union should be restricted to the confines of marriage and that marriage should be between a "biological man and woman." Throughout the United States, this was already becoming an outdated, minority view; however, in the more progressive states of Washington and Oregon, these teachings were considered highly offensive. Although the church continued to grow in weekend worship attendance, the public outcry against Western Shore intensified. Local politicians felt the pressure to do something to stop, "that big, bigoted, and backwards blight on our beautiful city."

In 2033, the Vancouver city council passed a resolution regarding hate speech. Similar to the LPA that would be passed over a decade later (in fact, much of the language from this resolution was used in the legislation adopted by Congress), this new law allowed the city to levy hefty fines against any speech, written or oral, which did not affirm the LGBTQ+ lifestyle.

Western Shore, assisted by an organization known as the *Center for Faith and Freedom*, challenged the law as violating their First Amendment rights. This case, *Western Shore v. Wilson,* went before the Supreme Court in May of 2035. In a 10-5 decision, the law was upheld on the grounds that one's free speech and religious freedom could not endanger the safety of others. Western Shore was among the first megachurches to disband their large public gatherings. After the passage of the LGBTQ+ Protection Act in 2046, other megachurches followed a similar pattern.

As well, the LPA made illegal any Christian media that didn't fully affirm LGBTQ+ individuals and their life decisions. Ambiguous references to God were allowed if they only mentioned God's love, hope, and the promise of life in heaven for everyone after death. Very few biblical references were allowed to be used in television and radio. Anything considered to be offensive or harmful—at the sole discretion of the FTC—would be disallowed.

These FTC powers also extended to the internet. A significant portion of the $800 billion annual funding for the enforcement of the LPA was allocated for sophisticated filters used to block sites originating in countries like Uganda and China. These nations targeted (and continue to target) American citizens with messages about God, the Bible, and what they call "the gospel." Most Americans believe that these are narrow-minded, unenlightened cultures promoting a dogmatic narrative regarding human nature and God's judgment of sin. Even with the highly advanced filters and artificial intelligence used by the FTC, many of these intolerant messages worm their way onto electronic devices in the United States.

In the years following the passage of LPA, numerous Christians began communicating on an alternative internet source, *The Light Web*. This illegal underground network has served and continues to serve as a bastion of nefarious activity and a venue for the promotion of false ideologies. Reportedly, individuals use *The Light Web* to share Bible verses and their erroneous beliefs regarding outdated religious ideas. While it is impossible to ascertain the exact number of websites and users of *The Light Web*, anecdotal reports indicate that more than a million individuals each week access content contained within this network.

The FTC has managed to keep these dangerous notions confined to the farthest corners of the internet. However, there continue to be repeated calls for Congress to provide even more funding for the FTC. Many believe that only through the hiring of additional agents and the development of more advanced detection software will this dangerous plague be eliminated from our society.

THE MUFFLED CHURCH

The technological changes occurring over the last half-century have also contributed greatly to the silencing of the church. Over this period, communication in our nation has become virtually all digital. Conversations are almost exclusively through electronic means. In 2068, *Harris Research* carefully monitored the daily activities of 2200 Americans for one month and determined the following:

> Ninety-eight percent of our communication today occurs with the assistance of some digital device. Older Americans text, post, and occasionally use a phone for a voice conversation. However, since the development of *Thrite*—the thought-to-text AI software developed in 2040—most younger Americans communicate their ideas, feelings, and opinions through their imaginations. Only 2 percent of our communication occurs without any digital medium. Hypothetically, if all our electronic devices ceased operating, we would effectively become a deaf/mute culture.

With the passage of the LPA in 2046, churches effectively became silenced. While Christians may be able to share their ideas through talking to another individual, this form of communication has become obsolete. It has become impractical in our modern world to share one's viewpoint without these notions traveling on the internet highway. LPA has, for the most part, provided the means to block these religious ideas from the forum of public debate. The legislation caused the Christian church in America to become further isolated from the mainstream culture.

The death of this antiquated institution was quickly drawing nigh.

CHAPTER 9

ET TU, BRUTE?

When the Attacks Turned on Affirming Churches

In February 2019, the professional tennis player Martina Navratilova wrote an op-ed in *The Sunday Times* in which she criticized collegiate sports for allowing transgender women to participate in female competitions. "Letting men compete as women," she wrote, "simply if they change their name and take hormones is unfair—no matter how those athletes may throw their weight around."[33]

Although Martina Navratilova was a lesbian and spokesperson for the LGBTQ+ movement, she was widely criticized for her comments and labeled "transphobic" by many in the media. *Athlete Ally*, an LGBTQ+ sports non-profit, decided to sever ties with Navratilova over her public statements.[34]

In 2029, Congressman Frank Harrison wrote an op-ed piece for the *New York Times,* extolling the benefits of monogamous relationships. Harrison, a homosexual and staunch political advocate for gay rights, wrote about his ten-year marriage to his husband, the adoption of their two children, the stability of their home life, and thankfulness for his partner's willingness to be a stay-at-home dad and caregiver for their children. While the congressman did not criticize any choices made by other individuals or families, the praise of his own lifestyle decisions received harsh criticism across various social media platforms. Many LGBTQ+ sympathizers called for an apology from the *New York Times*. One individual posted on social media the following rebuke of the congressman:

> While Mr. Harrison may think of himself as an advocate for our movement, in actuality, he wants to return our cause to the dark ages. His family life is reminiscent of "Leave It to Beaver;" it's just that Ward Cleaver is coming home to Jim instead of June. Seems that the congressman hasn't really advanced beyond the *LG* of the LGBTQ+ cause.

Navratilova and Harrison's public condemnations were examples of individuals who were previously accepted and praised by the LGBTQ+ movement, yet later discovered that their views on sexuality didn't change with the culture. Former allies found themselves criticized and "canceled" on social media. Once progressive advocates unexpectedly shifted to the camp of closed-minded "deplorables."[35] In other words, they simply couldn't or wouldn't change with the quickly shifting views of culture—a culture which suddenly turned on these former friends and demanded either allegiance or silence.

Attacked by Friends

In Act 3, scene 1 of William Shakespeare's play, *Julius Caesar*, the Roman dictator is assassinated by a group of senators. Among the assassins is Caesar's friend, Marcus Brutus. Upon realizing this fact, Caesar exclaims, "*Et tu, Brute?*," Latin for "also you, Brutus?" Julius Caesar could believe that others were attacking him, but not his friend. His question revealed the shock at the betrayal of this once loyal ally.

Beginning in the late 20s and continuing into the 30s and 40s, the Progressive Christian movement experienced a similar situation with the American culture. When social attitudes regarding marriage shifted in the early 2000s, mainline denominations adjusted their beliefs and practices. As same-sex marriage became legal in the United States, these more liberal churches began allowing same-sex weddings in their facilities. They permitted their clergy to officiate these ceremonies. They ordained into the ministry openly gay individuals. Same-sex relationships were viewed as morally equivalent to a "traditional" marriage between a person assigned as male at birth and a person assigned as female at birth.

These churches viewed themselves as being allies with the American culture. They placed rainbow banners on the outside of their buildings. Members of these churches regularly participated in LGBTQ+ parades and rallies. They locked arms with those whose beliefs about marriage and sexuality differed from the historical Christian teachings of the past. Whenever the media or celebrities attacked the Christian view of marriage, these churches were quick to differentiate their beliefs from those "other, fundamentalist churches."

Therefore, these progressive Christian churches believed they were safe from persecution. They were moral and political allies with the secularists. Progressive pastors and members of their churches firmly believed they would be exempt from the rising cultural and political persecutions.

However, the societal sands were shifting under their feet faster than they realized. LGBTQ+ advocates suddenly turned and thrust their knives into the backs of these liberal Christians. Congregations and Protestant denominations that had previously adapted to the cultural trends found themselves at odds with society's new norms. These formerly progressive, open-minded churches struggled to embrace the newest letters added to the ever-expanding, non-heterosexual acronym. Like certain actors, sports stars, and other celebrities, they simply couldn't keep up with the quickly changing morals of culture.

For example, throuples and other forms of polygamy are now considered morally acceptable relationships in America. However, for many years, this was not the case. It was only in 2022 that those who lived in these multi-partner relationships began to find legal recognition. In the case of *West 49th St., LLC v. O'Neill*, New York Civil Court Judge Karen May Bacdayan ruled that polyamorous relationships are entitled to the same sort of legal protection given to two-person relationships.[36] Numerous lower court cases followed in the coming years, forcing the Supreme Court to ultimately hear the case of *Mitchell/Smith/Holstead v. Watson* in 2036. The decision in 2033 by then President Warren to "pack" the court by appointing six additional, extremely liberal justices paved the way for rulings that agreed with these new norms. In *Watson*, the court ruled 10-5 that it was unconstitutional for any state to deny a marriage license to multiple partners. Following this decision, states were compelled to grant marriage licenses to threesomes, foursomes, or any other number of individuals wishing to marry.

The ruling was applauded most loudly in the state of Utah. Ironically, Utah was granted statehood in 1896 only after agreeing to no longer officially recognize polygamous marriages.[37] The year after this Supreme Court decision, Utah had ten times more applications for multi-partner marriages than the second-highest state, California.

The minority opinion pointed out the numerous future legal quandaries of this ruling. For example, members of criminal organizations could all marry, thus prohibiting a court from compelling them to testify against one another. There would be lawsuits regarding inheritances. When medical decisions needed to be made regarding a comatose individual who was in a polygamous relationship, which of the other partners would have the ultimate authority to decide? In the longest dissent in the history of the Supreme Court, Justice Brown highlighted the multiple legal predicaments that would come because of this ruling.

However, most of the justices believed that the government had no right to restrict the freedom of its citizens in the area of relationships and love. The language used in the majority opinion was similar to the 2015 *Obergefell v. Hodges* case, which ruled that any restriction on same-sex marriage was unconstitutional. Advocates for polygamous marriage hailed the *Mitchell/Smith/Holstead v. Watson* ruling as a "victory for love." They praised those justices as "understanding and elevating the right of every citizen to love in the way they see fit."

These difficult marital questions, though, eventually led to the decision in *Turner v. Wade* in 2059 to remove all marital privileges. Husbands and wives were stripped of all traditional spousal rights in every type of relationship: homosexual, heterosexual, or polygamous. Only a blood relative is now allowed to make a medical decision on behalf of a patient. If no blood relative exists or is willing to make such a decision, a *guardian ad litem*, appointed by the state, will decide what is best for the individual, sometimes contradicting the desires of the spouse or spouses.

The Supreme Court's majority opinion stated, in part: "the desire of this Supreme Court is that this ruling would not be used as a means for non-birthing persons to subjugate birthing-persons in marriages where there exists one non-birthing individual with multiple birthing-persons." However, practically speaking, this was the case in most multi-partner marriages. Even the more progressive churches in our country had trouble coming to terms with polygamy in general and polygamous marriages in particular. Many progressive churches believed this was a setback for the birthing-person's movement. As in the case with Martina Navratilova, these former allies of culture found themselves in the crosshairs of those in our country who wanted no relational or sexual boundaries.

A Bridge Too Far

Most progressive churches, as well, were unable to come to terms with the *Human Equality Act* of 2048, the legislation that banned any discrimination based on an individual's gender assigned at birth. HEA gave full recognition to the fluidity of gender. By this point in history, most in our culture rejected the notion that one's biological attributes determined the restrooms they used, or the sports teams open to them. HEA permitted biological males and biological females to participate without discrimination in any sporting event or activity, shower in any locker room, and join any fraternity, sorority, or civic club of their choosing. In a speech on the floor of Congress, Representative Terry Johnson-Smalls stated the following in support of this legislation:

> We have come so far in the movement for equal rights, yet we somehow haven't erased this last form of discrimination in our culture. We need no distinctions between the sexes. We are all just humans. Let's start acting that way!

Most liberal pastors and congregants believed HEA went too far. Progressive Christians argued that rather than providing protection against discrimination, this bill created a sexual free-for-all and situations where rape and sexual abuse would become more common. Moreover, many progressive pastors pointed to the detrimental effect of HEA on women's rights, particularly in the athletic world. Biological females simply could not compete against biological males. The loss of separate divisions for men's and women's sports effectively removed females from the athletic arena.

In the spring of 2048, a group of pastors from several mainline denominations gathered in Washington, D.C., to protest the passage of HEA. These pastors held meetings in which they discussed the legislation, explored options for action, and prayed together. As well, they met with numerous congresspersons, trying to convince them to vote against the HEA. Through various media outlets, they pleaded with Congress and the President to reject HEA and to create alternative legislation to protect the transsexual community from discrimination. Of course, their cries fell on deaf ears. During the summer of 2048, Congress passed and the President signed HEA into law.

In response, a progressive Christian pastor wrote the following:

I've always been a champion of the full rights of homosexuals. I celebrated when my denomination voted to allow clergy to perform same-sex marriage ceremonies. I took great pride when our church welcomed and affirmed openly gay and lesbian couples and individuals. I believed the old way of defining marriage was unfair to those with same-sex attraction. Why should they, just because of their sexual desires, be denied the same rights as the rest of us?

Except, this whole thing has really gone further than I ever imagined. Polygamy? I know some people are crying out for equal rights, but where does it end? Can five people all marry one another? 20? 500? 10,000?

And pedophilia? When and how did we start thinking that a 35-year-old man and a 12-year-old boy are okay?

And the whole transgender thing. About the time I was finally able to get comfortable with a biological male saying that they were actually female, and vice-versa, that entire notion became passé. Now, they are saying, "I dare you to define me." Gender was fluid. Now it's non-existent. Really?

We've gone from accepting to affirming to throwing out all common sense. I certainly don't want to go back to those narrow biblical definitions of marriage and sexuality, but at least there were *some* parameters. Now, the restraints are completely gone. Our culture has become a sexual *Lord of the Flies*.

Even more disconcerting for these progressive Christians was the dismantling of the previously accepted accommodations for two different genders. Prior to 2048, separate bathrooms for birthing persons and non-birthing persons existed in virtually all government buildings as well as private businesses. As offensive as it is to our modern sensibilities, these signs were commonly posted on doors leading into restroom facilities:

The HEA called for the removal of these and other offensive gender references in both the public and private sectors. No longer were people treated differently due to biological characteristics. The old rallying cry from many Christians of "separate but equal" wasn't convincing to most of our citizens. The only way to truly have equality was by eliminating these separate spaces.

Additionally, many Christians (both conservative and liberal) raised a primitive argument about the increase in sexual activity (including rape) by allowing all to use the same locker rooms and restrooms, and for members of the same teams to share hotel rooms. However, this assertion quickly crumbled with the counterargument that sexual activity is a natural, enjoyable function of the human body, and to restrict it is akin to disallowing individuals to eat, urinate, or yawn.

While progressive Christians had previously agreed with the culture that same-sex marriage should be an accepted practice in our nation, these same churches could not come to grips with these new norms. One pastor wrote in a blog dated July 12, 2045:

> I once thought of myself as a liberal. I celebrated the Obergefell decision. I wore a rainbow button. I believed that my LGBTQ+ neighbors had the right to enjoy the same privileges as the rest of society.
>
> However, I now find myself out of step with this movement. I believe that the LGBTQ+ movement was basically about equal rights. Perhaps that really was the case with some. But others simply desire permission for unfettered hedonism. They want to do whatever they want whenever they want. I'm not sure when self-restraint became a vice instead of a virtue, but it's easy to see the damage this is doing to our society. Much like the Roman Empire, we are going to crumble primarily because we implode from within.

As the cultural attitudes regarding sexual activity began to shift, so did the public perception of all Christians, regardless of whether they considered themselves to be conservative, moderate, or liberal. Christianity became, in the eyes of the culture, a social ill.

CHRISTIANITY AS A MENTAL DISORDER

For Progressive Christians, the clearest form of attack came from the medical community. Up until 1973, the American Psychiatric Association listed homosexuality as a mental disorder. From 1973 until 1986, it was considered to be a sexual disorder in those who were in conflict with their sexual orientation. In 1987, homosexuality was removed altogether from the *Diagnostic and Statistical Manual of Mental Disorders* (DSM).[38]

Somewhat ironically, in 2057—a mere seventy years after the removal of homosexuality from the DSM—the newly created Psychiatric Professionals of America voted overwhelmingly to add "Religious Faith" as a mental disorder. In a vote of 18,236 to 543, the members included this classification to the DSM-9 as a subcategory under schizophrenia. The conference attendees expressed their desire to help—not just condemn—those suffering from religious delusions. They noted that schizophrenia is a severe mental disorder in which the patient is unable to correctly interpret the reality of their environment. Those suffering from schizophrenia will exhibit a combination of hallucinations, delusions, and extremely disordered thinking, often impairing their ability to complete daily functions and appropriately relate to their environment.

Religious faith is a particular form of schizophrenia in which the patient believes in a god or gods and the existence of other

141

non-corporal spirits. Christianity is a common form of schizo-phrenia in the category of religious faith. Patients will most often exhibit abnormal beliefs about the creation of our world, about a so-called "resurrection" of a man named Jesus, and life after the physical death of the human body. Additionally, they will often claim to hear auditory messages from their "god," giving them directions for their lives (e.g., "God told me to accept this job, marry this person, talk with a coworker about my faith," etc.)

These individuals typically hold deviant beliefs on several issues, including sexuality, gender fluidity, abortion, and euthana-sia. They derive their values and moral code from this same "god" who, according to their beliefs, has given various commands dic-tating the behavior of humans. These guidelines are reportedly found in their religious book and are often quoted by individuals suffering from this form of schizophrenia.

An article in *Modern Psychology* outlined the best methods to use in assisting patients who hold these strong religious beliefs.

Treatment often includes a combination of antipsychotic medications as well as antidepressants or anti-anxiety drugs. Caregivers are advised that no one drug has proven effective across a wide spectrum of patients. Finding effec-tive prescriptions for individuals suffering from religious schizophrenia is often a result of trial and error.

As well, several cases of successful "deconstruction" therapies have been reported by some psychiatric profes-sionals. This process normally involves a rigorous six-to-nine-month in-patient treatment using a combination of group and individual therapy. The patients are asked to "prove" the existence of their "god" or other spiritual beings. They are given the opportunity to draw this "god" and then compare their drawings with others who claim to believe in this same "god." After months of studying the dissimilarities in their drawings, some come to realize that "god" is simply a creation of their own imaginations. More research is needed to determine the long-term viability of this treatment.

Even today, Americans are divided in their opinions on how to view Christians. The perspective of many mirrors that of the psychiatric community. According to those in this camp, these religious individuals need our help, not our condemnation.

However, many others disagree. Even if these religious notions do stem from mental illness, they argue, the ideas are dangerous to our society. As one writer noted, "Hitler may have been a mentally deranged madman, but I don't think the best way to deal with him would've been to give him a prescription and send him home." Those in this particular camp have pushed for stricter laws and harsher penalties for those who espouse these religious ideas.

Strange Bedfellows

The continued secularization of the American culture throughout the 30s, 40s, and 50s led to the alliance of former foes within American Christianity. Many Liberals, Progressives, Conservatives, and Fundamentalists found themselves uniting on a few key issues, chiefly around the idea of religious freedom.

Former "rivals" found themselves fighting a common foe. Even though they may have had strong disagreements with one another on a wide range of theological issues, all their existences were threatened by the continued secularization of America.

However, their efforts were ultimately in vain. The end of the church in America was quickly approaching. Joey Donavan, in an article he wrote just two years before his death, noted the following:

> Americans have essentially given God His walking papers. Our nation—founded on the tenets of the Judeo-Christian faith—has unquestionably rejected anything and everything to do with religion. I remember when our currency contained the phrase, *In God We Trust*. I remember when politicians would say, *God Bless America*. Those days are now gone. Sadly, *long, long gone*.

As most of the American population rejected the idea of anything beyond the natural world, state and local governments saw an open door to previously untapped revenues. The new tax laws passed by several state legislatures and local municipalities would become the death knell for many American churches. I cover this issue in the next chapter.

CHAPTER 10

THE POWER OF THE PURSE

How Property Taxes Crushed the Church

In a speech at the *Americans for Progress* annual convention in 2033, Senator James Smith famously quipped, "While we might not be able to legislate churches out of existence, we can damn sure tax them to death." The assembled crowd laughed and immediately shared this quote across multiple social media platforms. Senator Smith, a hero of the secular left, was leading the charge against "the religious fanatics and the fairy tales they continue to propagate upon our culture."

Those in attendance may have chuckled, but when Senator Smith's quote quickly spread throughout the social media world, church leaders shuttered. His statement wasn't a prediction; instead, it was a reality beginning to take shape in various communities across America.

In that same speech, the Vermont senator acknowledged the protections provided to churches by the United States Constitution yet praised the various state and municipal efforts to raise funds through taxing previously exempt religious organizations. In the early years of this century, many county governments asked churches to voluntarily make "PILOT" payments (Paid In Lieu Of Taxes). Although churches historically were exempt from property taxes, these counties applied sharp pressure on pastors and other religious leaders. Rumors began spreading that county commissioners were proposing to levy property taxes on churches. Other government officials wishing to avoid legal conflicts and possible public backlash offered a compromise: voluntary PILOT payments to the county appeased those officials wanting to fully tax churches and allowed these congregations to avoid paying the typically higher property tax rate.

But, in the 2030s, as the American attitude toward Christians took a decidedly negative turn, county officials across the nation became emboldened. They turned their attention toward this previously untapped revenue stream. PILOT payments were no longer accepted in counties and municipalities where, previously, this solution had served as an acceptable compromise. During the Second Great Recession of 2032, new laws swept across our nation. State and local governments, desperate for additional revenue streams, voted time and again to levy property taxes on church-owned buildings and land. In some cases, these churches were required to pay taxes at the "religious rate," a fee that was higher than a residential or commercial rate.

In a number of smaller, rural communities, especially in the southeastern region of the United States, local governments initially resisted levying these taxes against churches. Many of the county commissioners and school board officials either attended church or had parents and grandparents who had been active members of the churches in their community. Even if they rarely attended, many still possessed a generally favorable, often nostalgic, view of these churches. Their buildings and steeples were familiar, staple components of their community.

However, GR2 brought tremendous financial strain on local governments across the United States. These smaller communities reluctantly passed laws levying taxes on formerly exempt religious non-profits. In the years to come, these small towns would see many of their "firsts" disappear: First Methodist, First Baptist, First Presbyterian, First Christian, and other *First* churches, typically located within just a few blocks of one another, disbanded and sold their buildings.

The newly enacted laws were challenged in the courts. In some cases, these lower courts sided with the churches. Judges agreed that the religious freedom rights afforded by the United States Constitution could easily be stripped away simply through taxation. The so-called "separation of church and state" meant that neither entity could use its power to influence or hinder the normal operations of the other. Taxation would obviously be a means for the government to impede the activities of the church.

However, other lower courts sided with the state and local officials. They argued that property taxation did not violate the First Amendment; rather, it was both a right and a duty of government to tax entities within their jurisdiction to provide the necessary services for their residents. Since church members used roads and sidewalks to travel to their churches, they should be willing to pay taxes for these accommodations. These courts pointed to cases in which firefighters, police, and medical personnel responded to emergencies at church campuses. If churches didn't pay taxes—it was argued—then they should not expect civil assistance when their building caught fire or was burglarized.

With lower courts disagreeing on the matter, the United States Supreme Court ultimately decided to hear the case of *Smith v. Anchor*. The case centered on the County Treasurer of Orange County, California, Roselyn Smith, and Anchor Church, a large non-denominational church in Irvine, California. In March of 2034, the Orange County Commission introduced and passed a law requiring churches to pay property taxes at a "religious rate," which was 25 percent higher than commercial rates. The county informed the church of the new tax and, in the fall of 2034, sent a bill to the church offices. Anchor Church refused to pay the bill. When the county attempted to foreclose on the church property, Anchor hired an attorney and sued the county. The lower and appellate courts ruled in favor of Smith and Orange Country. The church appealed the case at each level. In the summer of 2036, the United States Supreme Court agreed to hear the case. The court sided with Smith and the county's right to tax religious organizations within its jurisdiction; however, the court also ruled that the county violated religious freedom in charging a higher "religious rate." Churches and other religious organizations could only be charged the universal commercial tax rate levied by the state or local government.

After 2036, *Smith v. Anchor* became the law of the land. By 2040, nearly every county in the United States had laws requiring churches to pay property taxes. In the late 30s and early 40s, thousands of churches sold or gave away their buildings. Smaller churches began meeting in the homes of church members. Many churches leased movie theaters or hotel ballrooms for their large gatherings. Some larger congregations managed to survive by selling portions of their land and buildings and then placing those funds in accounts designated for the payment of annual taxes owed.

These changes in the law produced three immediate outcomes. First, to the casual observer, it seemed that churches disappeared from the national landscape relatively quickly. For decades, many small towns and communities had a church on every corner. Steeples dotted the skyline of almost all small towns. Within half a generation, these buildings had either been renovated or demolished. Restaurants, bars, theaters, retail shops, and condos took their places. The heavy taxes imposed upon them effectively removed most churches from the public eye.

Second, while the members of these churches continued to meet in homes or rented spaces, these churches lost one of their chief outreach tools. Previously, individuals would come to these churches out of curiosity, searching for counseling or help with a financial or other need. The convenience of the church location made it easy for these seekers to wander into a service or attend an event on the church campus. The sudden loss of these once conspicuous buildings made it virtually impossible for a stranger to find gatherings of Christians in their community.

Third, the churches that could pay the newly instituted taxes were only able to do so through a major reduction of spending in their ministries. The first and deepest cut was in their support of mission efforts. These churches dramatically decreased or stopped altogether their giving to national and international mission organizations. They stopped supporting local charities—such as homeless shelters or addiction recovery centers. Any funds allocated for ministries outside the church were diverted to pay these property tax bills.

When these reductions weren't enough, they decreased spending on ministries within the church. Budgets for camps, retreats, teaching supplies, musical equipment, and furnishings were dramatically reduced. Staff and volunteers were told to simply make do with what they had. There just wasn't money available for more.

Then came salary reductions and personnel layoffs. Many pastors were already struggling financially after the IRS eliminated the clergy housing allowance in 2028. The rule dated back to 1921 (applying only to church-owned parsonages) and was expanded in 1954 to include housing owned or rented by pastors.[39] This IRS provision allowed ordained pastors to designate a portion of their salary as housing and shelter this amount from federal and state taxes. This law effectively provided additional compensation to pastors in the form of a significant reduction in taxes owed to the IRS.

However, this rule had been challenged on numerous occasions, and in 2028 the IRS determined that this allowance did provide an unfair advantage to religious professionals and therefore served as a "governmental support of and entanglement with religion." The change in this tax law added a financial burden to pastors, including many who were serving in churches with declining offerings.

The new property tax bills made it even more challenging for churches to employ pastors in a full-time capacity. Both pastoral and non-pastoral staff members were terminated. Utilities, essential services, and property taxes were non-negotiable. Everything else customarily included in a church budget was subject to reduction or complete elimination.

How New Taxes Destroyed an Old Church

A blog post by a former pastoral staff member at Christ Church of Charlotte, North Carolina, described the effect of these new taxes on the missions and ministries of their church. In a post dated June 1, 2045, the author explained how the church campus sat in the downtown business district of the city for over two hundred years. In 2037, the county government voted to assess property taxes on churches at the usual commercial millage rate of .0390. The nearly ten acres of property owned by Christ Church was valued at just under $40 million. The annual property tax bill amounted to over $1.5 million. Nearly half the church's annual budget would go to pay property taxes.

The first year they received a property tax bill, the church immediately entered into crisis mode. Their annual Christmas musical was attended by a couple of thousand people each year. The church did not charge for tickets, even though it cost nearly $50,000 for the rental equipment and stage design. According to this pastor, it was the church's gift to the community, and they enjoyed blessing their neighbors in this manner. However, it was no longer feasible. The Finance Committee quickly cut this musical from the budget.

Church leaders tried everything they could not to let personnel go. They cut funding for ministries dramatically. Pastors canceled annual children and student summer camps. Vacation

Bible School—a free week-long morning camp for kids—had been an annual tradition of the church for nearly a century. It was no more. Retreats, dinners, and church events were eliminated, or their budgets cut so low that they would only be a shadow of their previous form.

As well, all giving to missions ceased. Prior to 2045, Christ Church gave $200,000-$300,000 annually to various charitable organizations. Nearly $150,000 was allocated for support of overseas mission work. As well, the church was a large financial contributor to the budgets of a homeless shelter, a battered women's shelter, and a halfway house for newly released prisoners. While many church members continued volunteering in those places, all financial support from the church ceased. Those funds now went to pay the enormous property tax bill.

This pastor's blog noted that, initially, some members complained about the leadership's decision to cut funding to those organizations. Those individuals who volunteered in these local ministries saw the positive effects of the dollars given. But, when made aware of the financial situation, they understood. When faced with a seven-figure tax bill, what else could the church do?

The Finance Team worked on numerous creative ways to reduce expenses without having to lay off personnel. However, the math wouldn't work. According to this pastor:

> At the end of the day, it still wasn't enough. Several staff members lost their jobs. Including me. Initially, I was shocked and angry. Except, when I saw the drastic cuts in the budget, I knew there were no other options. We simply could not pay that property tax bill and continue

to operate in the same way. It was a new day for Christ Church and churches throughout our nation.

The blog further explained that in addition to the tax bill, the county instituted a one-time transfer tax of 20 percent whenever a property used for religious worship services was sold and used for commercial purposes. Other municipalities had adopted a similar tax policy. The argument made by the county was that a church typically held meetings only once or twice a week, while commercial businesses would have clients and customers coming and going throughout the week, thus requiring more government services. This transfer tax would help pay for these additional costs to the county.

Eventually, Christ Church was forced to sell their property, pay the transfer tax, and use the funds to lease a facility in a neighboring county. However, many members could no longer join the worship gatherings due to the distance from their homes to the new campus. The church membership and attendance numbers fell substantially over the next ten years until the church finally dissolved in 2045.

These new taxes did exactly what they were designed to do: they pushed churches into the shadows and limited the funds they could use to teach and spread their message. Across America, steeples disappeared from cities and towns. Church buildings were no longer part of the American landscape. Churches were forced—through taxation—to close their doors forever.

Senator James Smith was partially right. To the casual observer, it did appear that these new taxes finally killed the church. But taxes alone would not have been sufficient to bring about the death of the church in America. Throughout the history of Christianity, many local churches never owned property. While most Americans picture a *church* as a building or a campus, the historical documents I found use this word to define a group of Christians who commit themselves to one another and their god. In the nearly 2100-year history of Christianity, hundreds of thousands—perhaps *millions*—of churches have existed without the luxury of owning communal property for the purpose of worship and other gatherings. Many churches have thrived while meeting in homes of members, rented spaces, or in outdoor public spaces. Even today, in many places around the world, this is a reality for countless numbers of churches.

While the enactment of property tax laws proved to be a substantial wound to the church in America, I believe it could have survived this attack. In fact, the American church might very well still be alive today, even with the loss of buildings and campuses.

Except, more persecution was coming.

Much more.

CHAPTER 11

TAKE THIS JOB

When Christians Were Excluded from the Workforce

In 2022, an actor named Kirk Cameron wrote a children's book entitled *As You Grow*. Cameron—a 1980s teen heartthrob and star of a popular sitcom—was also outspoken about his Christian faith. As was a common practice at that time, Cameron's publisher contacted numerous public libraries about the author using their space to host a program for local children. The author would come, read from their book to the children, and then offer free copies along with crafts or other activities associated with the book. Authors used these events to generate publicity for their books, but they were free for children and their families.

Cameron's publisher sent emails to several public libraries extending this opportunity to host a well-known actor and author in their space. However, because of the Christian focus of the book, these public libraries declined the offer. According to one article:

...over 50 public libraries have either outright rejected him or not responded to requests on his behalf... Many of the same libraries that won't give Cameron a slot, however, are actively offering "drag queen" story hours or similar programs for kids and young people, according to Cameron's book publisher and according to a review of the libraries' websites and current program listings.[40]

Cameron's story certainly wasn't unique. In the 2010s and 20s, Christians slowly became marginalized in the workplace. In 2013, a Christian husband-and-wife bakery shop team in Oregon declined to bake a wedding cake for a lesbian couple. The bakery owners recommended other bakery shops and were willing to sell any of their baked goods to this same-sex couple; however, the crafting of a cake specifically designed for a same-sex marriage ceremony violated their religious beliefs. Although this husband-and-wife team hoped for a "you go your way and I'll go mine" solution to this dilemma, their retail shop was hounded by gay rights activists. Eventually, they were forced to close their business.[41]

In 2015, The Christian owners of Görtz Haus Gallery in Grimes, Iowa, had to close their business entirely after they were charged with discrimination for refusing to hold a same-sex wedding at the venue. Richard Odgaard and his wife, Betty, were forced to close their business, a gift shop, bistro, and wedding venue, two years after they told a gay couple from Des Moines their facility couldn't host a same-sex wedding. When local news reported the discrimination complaint, other couples canceled their bookings. The Odgaards were forced to pay a $5,000 settlement for their refusal to hold a same-sex marriage ceremony. Rather than continue to face fines and harassment, the couple sold their building to a church.[42]

During the COVID-19 pandemic, Samaritan's Purse opened a volunteer field hospital in New York City's Central Park to help care for patients. Staff and volunteers at this hospital were required to sign a statement of faith which read, in part, "We believe that marriage is exclusively the union of one genetic male and one genetic female" and "Human life is sacred from conception to its natural end." The decision to allow this organization to operate in New York drew protests from activists and politicians. State Senator Brad Hoylman stated, "I do fear that we've given Franklin Graham [the CEO of Samaritan's Purse] a platform in one of the most famous pieces of public land in the country to spew his hatred of LGBTQ people, and unfortunately at the same time legitimize his homophobia." Before actions to remove this charitable organization could be taken, the field hospital operation ceased.[43]

In 2023, an Arizona school board voted to dissolve a five-year partnership with Arizona Christian University due to a concern over the school's publicly stated beliefs. School board members expressed their dismay over the hiring of teachers receiving degrees whose mission is to "transform the culture with truth by promoting the biblically informed values that are foundational to Western civilization, including the centrality of family, traditional sexual morality, and lifelong marriage between one man and one woman." The board also stated a desire to evaluate the beliefs of teachers to ensure that those of other religions and those in the LGBTQ+ community would feel safe in their presence.[44]

Recognition, Rights, Acceptance, and Affirmation

Throughout the 2020s and 30s, the American culture continued to apply tremendous pressure on Christians to affirm lifestyle and moral choices that contradicted their historical beliefs. It was not enough to accept and show kindness to someone, even if you disagreed with their relationship decisions. At this point in America's history, society demanded that Christians affirm the equal validity of all sexual and marriage relationships, whether heterosexual, homosexual, or otherwise.

This new reality manifested itself throughout our culture and nowhere more so than in the business and commercial sectors of our nation. The progression of demands by the LGBTQ+ community regarding labor rights can be summarized in the following manner:

1970s-80s: We demand the right to be "out." Gay and lesbian citizens of our nation shouldn't have to hide in the shadows. It's a travesty that an actor like Rock Hudson had to keep his homosexuality hidden, fearing that he would not receive leading roles if the public knew about his same-sex relationships. Gay and lesbian lawyers, bankers, teachers, and plumbers should feel the freedom to be open about who they are without facing persecution.

1990s-2010s: We demand equal rights. We believe corporations should be required to offer the same benefits to partners in same-sex relationships that are given to married couples, including health coverage and insurance benefits. We believe states should recognize same-sex marriages and offer the same legal, financial, and medical advantages afforded to spouses in heterosexual marriages.

2020s-2030s: We demand all businesses offer their services to us, regardless of the owner's religious beliefs. Even if we could secure those services through another retail establishment, we will force you to violate your conscience through social and legal pressure.

2040s-50s: We demand your acquiescence to certain beliefs if you want to be employed or do business within our society. We will force you to sign a statement of beliefs in which you state your agreement to the moral equality of all relationships and the equal validity of all religious beliefs.

During this seventy-year period, Christians struggled with navigating these evolving workplace demands. However, the 20s, 30s, and 40s proved to be especially challenging for Christians in the workforce. Most felt caught between wanting to provide for their families and remaining true to their beliefs.

Initially, Christians fought these requirements through legal avenues. Throughout the decade of the 2030s, there were numerous court battles, all with the same theme: *How does a society allow religious freedom while protecting the rights of its citizens?* Legal scholars debated (incessantly) the unresolvable tension between these two rights. How can a Christian teacher who is morally opposed to homosexual relationships treat fairly a student who is openly gay? How can a Christian attorney adequately represent a client if that attorney believes this client is acting in ways that are an "abomination to God?"[45] Can a Christian doctor honestly treat, to the best of their ability, an LGBTQ+ patient?

In the first half of the 2030s, several lower courts issued contradicting opinions on this question. While each had their various nuances, they all leaned either in support of religious freedom or in support of individual rights. Each time, one "right" would supersede the other. If the Christian's religious freedom were upheld, the rights of the individual were violated. If the rights of the individual were prioritized, the rights of religious freedom and expression of that freedom were diminished. Every case seemed to mirror the old physics conundrum of *what happens when an unstoppable force hits an immovable object?* There was simply no way both "rights" could coexist in our culture. Either the unstoppable force would be stopped, or the immovable object would be moved. There was just no other option.

THE *HYPOCRITICAL* OATH?

In the summer of 2038, the United States Supreme Court finally answered this question with the decision handed down in *Wright v. Brookdale Medical Systems.* Dr. Dennis Wright, a general surgeon in Birmingham, Alabama, refused to sign the *Patient Rights and Affirmation Pledge* (PRAP) introduced in January of 2037 by the Brookdale Medical Systems. Signing PRAP was required for all employees and medical personnel using the hospital facilities. PRAP, in essence, outlined the rights of patients and specifically highlighted equal treatment regardless of a patient's sexual identity or lifestyle. Included in this document was language regarding the moral beliefs of those providing care. Dr. Wright refused to sign the Brookdale PRAP because of wording used in one specific section of the document:

Understanding that beliefs determine behavior, I recognize the moral validity of any sexual choice, lifestyle, or gender identification. Exclusive, narrow-minded views will inevitably lead to certain negative actions, including but not limited to micro-aggressions, passive non-treatment, or even willful neglect of a patient. I pledge to provide fair and equal care to every patient in Brookdale Medical Systems and to do so through a careful adherence to beliefs that acknowledge the moral equivalency of heterosexual, homosexual, bi-sexual, polyamorous, hebephilia, ephebophilia, pansexual, skoliosexual, spectrasexual, and other "non-traditional" sexual choices and lifestyles. I recognize that any belief regarding the moral superiority of a particular sexual attraction and choice is inherently discriminatory and will invariably affect my ability to provide the best care and treatment for clients of Brookdale Medical Systems. Should my beliefs on the issue of sexuality change, I will immediately notify the Director of Inclusion or, if they are unavailable, the CEO of Brookdale Medical Systems. This notification may result in a refusal of facility use, suspension, requirement of tolerance training, or termination.

Dr. Wright, a professing Christian and active member of a large Presbyterian church in Birmingham, refused to sign the PRAP document precisely because of the language in the paragraph above. As a result, Brookdale Medical Systems denied Dr. Wright any future hospital privileges. This move meant Dr. Wright was denied access to the surgical facilities of the hospitals in the Birmingham area and, therefore, was unable to perform surgeries for most of his patients.

Dr. Wright immediately filed a lawsuit against Brookdale Medical Systems. His attorney argued that Dr. Wright was, in fact, able to offer complete and equal care to every patient, regardless of his personal religious beliefs. Requiring employees or physicians using the facilities to deny their sincerely held religious beliefs was both a historical first and a violation of their constitutional rights.

Dr. Wright's attorney filed the lawsuit in the Northern Alabama Federal District Court in February 2037. Dr. Wright won the case. The court agreed with his attorney's argument that Dr. Wright's religious liberties were, in fact, violated by the language in PRAP. Immediately, PRAP was suspended, and Dr. Wright was allowed to use the hospital facilities.

However, Brookdale Medical Systems appealed the decision to the Fifth Circuit Court. This time, the court sided with the hospital system and reversed the lower court decision. PRAP, however, remained suspended as the appellate court anticipated the resulting appeal to the United States Supreme Court.

Finally, the stage was set. Corporations, labor unions, and other employee organizations were anxious to have this matter settled. Could an employer require any employee to hold certain beliefs as a condition for employment? Would religious freedom trump individual rights, or would individual rights win the day?

In a 10-5 decision, the Supreme Court upheld the decision of the appellate court. The majority opinion offered, in part, the following argument for elevating individual rights over religious freedom:

For far too many years, so-called "religious freedoms" have been used as a shield for blatant discrimination. Less than a century ago, many in our nation used the Christian Bible in support of their racist and antisemitic views. Over the last several decades, similar language has been used in defense of beliefs regarding sexual practices outside of a "traditional" marriage relationship. While this court recognizes the rights of our citizens to believe in and worship as they choose, this religious freedom cannot serve as a cover for bigotry. Love is love, and every reasonable member of society understands this truth. Even a privately held belief to the contrary will invariably harm others. Therefore, Christians who work for public and private institutions can and should be required to align their beliefs with the business, organization, or government. Certainly, they retain the freedom to worship as they choose; however, this worship cannot perpetuate hatred. Any individual who agrees to treat everyone with respect yet believes that same-sex marriage is immoral is a walking contradiction. That simply cannot be tolerated if our nation is to truly be a place of freedom and equality for all citizens.

This SCOTUS decision paved the way for a near-universal adoption of PRAP by hospitals and medical systems across the nation. Much like HIPPA (Health Insurance Portability and Accountability Act) enacted in the late 1990s and early 2000s, PRAP is today acknowledged by the medical community as an essential tool for providing patients with the best medical care.

While there were initial challenges to *Wright*—for the last thirty years—this has been the law of the land.

Moreover, PRAP paved the way for similar requirements in both public and private sectors. In 2042, Congress passed the *Students and Teachers Right to Equal Education and Treatment* (STREET) Act. This legislation required all teachers, administrators, and other workers in any school receiving federal money to sign a pledge similar to PRAP. There were numerous challenges to this legislation; however, the courts refused to hear the cases and referred to *Wright* as settled law.

In 2044, Congress passed the *Marketplace Equality and Protections Act* (MEPA), which enabled customers and clients to file complaints against any business that discriminated against sexual choices in the practices or beliefs of owners or employees. This legislation was based upon previously passed SOGI (Sexual Orientation and Gender Identity) legislation but added protections from the beliefs of owners and employees and provided an expeditious path for filing complaints against a business.

By 2045, virtually all major corporations in the United States adopted language like that used for PRAP in their employee handbooks. Employees were and are required to sign agreements to these pledges as a condition for employment.

After nearly 80 years of discussions, debates, compromises, and numerous court cases, the issue was finally settled. The so-called religious rights of Christians could not bleed over into any form of discrimination. While the Constitution protects one's right to worship a god or gods, this right does not grant the freedom to hold prejudicial views toward other members of society. Christians may have been disappointed with this guiding principle; however, they could not claim to misunderstand the stance of the courts. Ambiguity gave way to clarity. Our culture would no longer tolerate abhorrent beliefs wrapped in the protective bubble of religious freedom.

Jesus or a Paycheck?

By the late 2040s, Christians were faced with three choices: 1) lie and hide their true beliefs regarding sexuality and gender orientation, 2) change their beliefs regarding sexuality and gender orientation, or 3) find a way to provide for their families without working for a major corporation or a business subject to the requirements of MEPA.

Option three was, understandably, an arduous task. The reach of MEPA was far and wide. For several years, Christians found ways to work in Christian-owned companies that only did business with other Christians. They avoided complaints by attempting to restrict their commercial relationships to those who agreed with their beliefs. However, this, too, proved to be a virtually impossible path forward. These business owners dealt with suppliers who were not Christian, and any of these vendors were potentially able to file a complaint. Unknown and unvetted customers or clients were always threats. This underground network of Christian businesses still exists today; however, these black-market goods and services represent a minuscule portion of the American economy.

This inability of Christians to provide for their family served as a tremendous blow to Christianity in America. The death of the church, I'm convinced, would not have occurred without this attack on Christians and their fundamentalist beliefs. The enactment of PRAP and the similar laws that followed had three major effects on the church in America.

First, these new laws effectively pushed Christians into the lower socio-economic class of our nation. This group lost their previously held political influence. At one time, Christians occupied the highest offices of our government. Obviously, this is no longer the case. The Christian voice in our national dialogue has been muted.

As well, Christians lost any financial leverage in the business world. For most of our nation's history, there have existed highly successful Christian businessmen and women, CEOs, and entrepreneurs. Christians have, in previous times, owned extremely profitable fast-food chains, retail establishments, financial institutions, and other businesses and corporations. Today, with these new laws, these individuals can no longer serve in these positions.

Second, numbers of Christians chose to abandon their faith. One archived blog contained the following confession:

> I'm caught between a rock and a hard place. It's either my beliefs about Jesus or providing for my family. I choose the latter. A Christian friend quoted that verse to me: "Demas, because he loves the things of this world, has abandoned us." Yeah, I love to see my children eat. What is wrong with that?

Some Christians claimed they were able to both sign the various tolerance pledges and remain true to their commitment. However, as these laws have become increasingly more specific about beliefs, the "both/and" option is virtually impossible. It is today—quite clearly—either Jesus or the job. One must choose, and many Christians chose to abandon their faith for a paycheck.

The third major effect of these laws is that there are now almost no adult converts to Christianity. While this is difficult to quantify (if someone does become a Christian, they certainly do not share this with others), the anecdotal evidence is strong. What occurred frequently in years past is no longer the case today. For much of America's history, adults embracing the Christian faith was not uncommon. At events called "revivals" or "crusades," hundreds—perhaps even thousands—of men and women would publicly proclaim their newfound commitment to Jesus. Now, however, the cost of that decision is just too great. A conversion to Christ means the loss of a job, social standing, and potentially family and friends. Most adults refuse to even consider that option.

It is impossible to overstate the significance of these labor laws in bringing about the end of the church in America. Even so, it was not the deadliest weapon used to eradicate the church. To exterminate Christianity from our culture, there had to be a particular focus on the younger generation. This final thread—the one that ultimately hammered the proverbial nail in the coffin of the church—is covered in the next chapter.

CHAPTER 12

JESUS AND NO LITTLE CHILDREN

The End of Christian Education

In February 2023, a public school teacher in Auburn, Washington posted about her school district's need to protect student's privacy rights. This teacher wrote: "So many students are not safe in this nation from their Christo-fascist parents. And our guidelines and laws haven't caught up with this."[46]

Initially, this teacher was heavily criticized by numerous conservative media outlets. However, within a decade after these comments were posted, most Americans polled agreed with these sentiments. The majority of citizens wanted to prevent one generation from passing to the next generation their religious dogmas and fantasies about a god or gods, heaven, hell, and bodies having souls that last beyond physical death. Throughout the 30s and 40s, calls grew for stricter guidelines and regulations to protect children from the influence of their parents.

Moreover, educators began keeping their fingers on the religious pulse of teachers and administrators. Accounts of middle and high school biology teachers giving instruction on evolution—but with a wink and a nod telling their students, "There is also the possibility that humans arrived on this earth through *creation*"—became far too common. Other reports described history teachers explaining, without any filters, the religious views of Martin Luther and the impact of the Protestant Reformation on the European economy and governments. As well, there were whispers and rumors of teachers talking with individual students about their religious beliefs. While government schools were purportedly free from religious ideas, Christian educators had historically been allowed a great deal of freedom in bringing their private beliefs into the public sphere.

Most American citizens understood the need to protect our nation's children and ensure the future well-being of our society. As the former Secretary of Education, Julie Hardin-Smalls, stated in September 2040:

> If teachers want to worship God or Jesus or Buddha on their own time, I don't care. However, under this administration, we will be sure to ask the right questions of anyone applying to work in our school systems. If their beliefs contradict scientifically proven facts regarding evolution or any other known reality, they will not receive a job offer. If current teachers hold views contrary to these facts, we will not renew contracts. Furthermore, I promise you that we will work tirelessly to ensure that no student is exposed to teachings and ideas that not only go against human reason but promote a system of morals contrary to the beliefs of our nation.

Throughout the 30s and 40s—in reaction to the hard-line stance of the public school systems across the nation—Christian private schools exploded in growth. Many Christian teachers who were unwilling to change their religious beliefs found employment in these schools. Christian families prioritized budgets to pay their children's tuition fees. The number of homeschooled children more than tripled from 2025 to 2045. During this same twenty-year period, public school enrollment in this nation declined by half, from nearly 50 million students to just under 25 million. Families who wanted a Christian education for their children were generally able to afford the cost due to laws passed by almost two dozen states in the earlier part of this century—namely, legislation that allowed public money to fund private education.

The Nation's Near-Fatal Misstep

In the 20s, numerous states and local municipalities approved laws allowing parents—particularly in what were described as "failing schools"—to enroll their child in a private school and to use public tax dollars to pay all or a portion of the tuition. Most parents initially chose to send their children to private Christian schools, thus exposing them to religious ideas. Throughout the 2020s and 30s, as overall church attendance declined, the enrollment in private schools more than doubled.

However, by 2035, public sentiment shifted regarding public funds being used to indoctrinate children. Most states passed laws prohibiting these schools from requiring students to participate in religious activities. Under these new guidelines, students could opt out of any required chapel services or religious instruction classes. These laws were challenged in the courts, and ultimately, the Supreme Court's decision in 2038 (*Veritas Academy v. Pennsylvania*) settled the matter. If the private school accepted any public money, the school could not force any religious instruction or activity upon a student.

Even with this provision in place, state legislators understood the perils of allowing these schools to influence the views of our youngest generation. While parents did have the option of withdrawing their children from religious classes, some did not take advantage of this provision. An archived parenting blog entitled, *What I Did Wrong,* revealed the feelings of one particular parent and likely represented many others whose children fell victim to the dangers of Christian private education. This mom described her excitement when the state of Georgia passed the School Choice Act, offering $6500 per child for tuition at a private school. Her seventh-grade daughter was in a severely failing public middle school. Virtually every week, Mom received an email from the vice-principal alerting parents that the police were called because of a fight involving weapons, because drugs were discovered, or because some student seriously threatened a teacher or administrator. According to Mom, her daughter wasn't learning anything other than how to cuss like a sailor, the street names for illegal drugs, and the A-Zs of sex. As a single mom, she couldn't quit her job to homeschool her daughter, and—before the School Choice Act—she simply couldn't afford private education.

But, with this tuition assistance program in place, Mom was able to enroll her daughter in a local Christian private school.

While she disagreed with the stated religious beliefs of the school, she figured her daughter could just ignore those teachings that weren't in line with normally accepted viewpoints. It was a better school and a better education for her daughter, and Mom simply felt like she had no other option.

But, when her daughter came home one evening and revealed that she had become a Christian that day, this mom realized her mistake. She wrote:

I won't bore you with all the details of our long conversation that followed. Let's just say it was extensive, emotional, and not very productive. My daughter had fallen victim to the fanatical side of this otherwise (mostly) good school. I probably should have seen this coming, but I thought my highly intelligent girl would be able to eat the fish and spit out the bones of this private school education. Apparently, though, she could not separate the bad from the good. So, I had no choice. I pulled her from this private school and placed her back in her former public school. Many, many fights between the two of us followed this decision.

What do I regret? Moving her to this private Christian school in the first place. I should have known better. I should have done a more thorough job of researching their religious teachings. Now, my daughter and I are having to live with the consequences of my foolish decision.

Other similar stories and accounts of indoctrination surfaced throughout the late 30s and early 40s, causing most state legislatures to either radically change or eliminate the school choice options for parents.

In 2041, Congress passed the *Protecting Our Kids Against Religious Dogma* Act (POKARD), which placed strict regulations on the language used and classes offered by private schools, including private Christian schools. POKARD protects all students under eighteen from being subjected to religious courses or activities, including religious chapels. This legislation essentially standardized education across the public and private sectors, with exceptions given to any students who are legal adults and opt to participate in these religious activities.

POKARD has been instrumental in protecting students from the religious instruction of teachers or administrators who secretly hold obsolete religious beliefs. Ideas of heaven, hell, and a need to believe in absolute truths for so-called "salvation" have been virtually eliminated from public and private classrooms. Moral dogmas are no longer thrust upon vulnerable, impressionable minds. Since the 2040s, these false ideologies have been unable to find a home within America's educational system.

Understanding this new reality, many Christian parents attempted an alternative method of education for their children. Initially, their efforts succeeded and gained a significant foothold across this country. However, our nation managed to face this new threat with similar, decisive legislation.

Homeschool Expansion and Death

From the early 1990s through 2019, homeschooling in the United States grew at a steady, substantial rate, normally around 2-8 percent per year. However, during the COVID pandemic of 2020 and the years following, homeschool enrollment experienced a meteoric explosion. From 2019 to 2021, the number of homeschooled students in our nation grew by almost 50 percent, from approximately 1.5 million students to as many as 2.7 million students.[47]

This dramatic rise in homeschooling caused concern among our nation's government and institutions of higher education. In an archived article from October 2023, a writer from the *Washington Post* offered the following warning:

> Many of America's new home-schooled children have entered a world where no government official will ever check on what, or how well, they are being taught.
> "Policymakers should think, 'Wow — this is a lot of kids,'" said Elizabeth Bartholet, an emeritus professor at Harvard Law School and child welfare advocate. "We should worry about whether they're learning anything."[48]

The sentiments expressed by Bartholet in 2023 grew exponentially in the following years. With more and more families choosing this homeschooling option, the eyes of government and education officials turned to monitoring these homeschooling parents and networks.

In the 2040s, numerous states—particularly those in the Northeast and on the West Coast—banned homeschooling as an option for their residents. Students were required to attend a state-authorized school. Homeschool networks, typically comprised of homeschool parents teaching their children together in church classrooms, did not meet the qualifications necessary to be approved by the states. Families whose children did not register for and attend school were visited by truancy officers. In most states, a warning and/or a fine proceeded the child being removed from the home and placed with child-protective services.

In the aftermath of these new state laws, many households moved to homeschool-friendly states. Florida became the "go-to" state for homeschooling families. From 2045-46, real estate prices increased by 25-40 percent throughout Florida due to this population boom. Conversely, in those states that banned homeschooling, homeowners saw sharp decreases in the value of their houses as the market became flooded with available properties.

This massive migration and the resulting housing crisis created enormous pressure on Congress to introduce legislation that brought equity to our nation's educational systems. In 2048, Congress passed a series of laws that effectively banned homeschooling in all fifty states. Exceptions for children with physical or mental handicaps were allowed; however, the process of acquiring waivers was extremely difficult and burdensome. Today, only a minuscule percentage of children are educated in their homes.

It took twenty years, but the hopes and desires of the Auburn public school teacher in 2023 were finally realized. America's laws and guidelines have, indeed, "caught up with our need to protect children from the few remaining Christo-fascist parents in our country." Curtailing parents' attempts to indoctrinate their children with religious fantasies has considerably diminished the

Christian population of our nation. Preventing a generation from inheriting the beliefs of former generations served as an essential tool in changing the religious landscape of America.

KILLING CHRISTIAN HIGHER EDUCATION

In October 2023, the U.S. Department of Education levied a $37.7 million fine against Grand Canyon University—an openly Christian, private school—for lying to "more than 7,500 former and current students about the cost of its doctoral programs over several years."[49] The USDE did acknowledge the fact that GCU offered disclosures to prospective students explaining the additional costs for continuation courses—which are often required for the completion of a doctoral program. However, the agency believed these disclosures were not sufficient to explain the higher fees paid by a majority of doctoral students.

In 2016, the Department of Education fined Penn State University $2.4 million for failing to report crimes on its campus by Jerry Sandusky, who was convicted in 2012 of abusing ten boys, many in Penn State's football locker room.[50] In 2019, the USDE levied a $4.5 million fine against Michigan State University for its "systemic failure" to address the sexual abuse committed by Larry Nassar, the MSU and USA Gymnastics doctor who admitted to sexually assaulting his patients for decades.[51]

The contrast in fines levied (nearly $38 million for GCU compared with $2.4 million and $4.5 million for Penn State and MSU respectively) was a harbinger of things to come for Christian higher education. Private Christian colleges and universities continued to face financial and social pressures in the coming years, especially as the cultural winds blew hard against religious freedom in favor of a more secularized society.

In 2033, the Higher Education Tuition Reduction Act (HETRA) made it possible for 95 percent of students to attend any state college or university at virtually no cost to that student or their family. Like the plan initially proposed by Senator Bernie Sanders ten years earlier, this legislation called on the federal government to provide an additional $60 billion per year to fund education for any student attending a public two-year community college or four-year college. The federal partnership with states has allowed most students today to attend college tuition-free. No monies, however, have been allotted for private higher education.

HETRA, in combination with increased scrutiny on private Christian education, made it virtually impossible for Christian colleges and universities to remain solvent. While a few private schools with large endowments have maintained a steady level of student enrollment, most Christian schools have closed their doors since the adoption of HETRA.

As the cultural attitudes toward Christianity soured, so did the desire for Christian higher education. Applications for admittance to most Christian schools steadily decreased as potential students gravitated toward less-expensive and less-religious options.

Just as Hardin-Smalls explained years earlier, preventing one generation from passing their religious dogmas to the next generation quickly eradicated Christianity in the United States. Over the next decade, the number of individuals in their 20s who regularly attended church plummeted. The average age in Christian churches was steadily increasing *before* these restrictions were placed on Christian private schools and homeschooling. After these new laws went into effect, the graying of congregations grew dramatically. Most pastors could look around on a Sunday morning and surmise that they were just a few funerals away from having to close the doors to the church forever.

And they were right.

LIFE AFTER DEATH

The State of America a Decade Later

Unquestionably, the founders of our nation believed in the religious dogmas of the Judeo-Christian tradition. As a historian, it is impossible to deny the impact and influence of the Christian church in the building of this country. The United States Constitution, the Bill of Rights, and most of the laws first established were written by those who held a Christian or, minimally, a monotheistic worldview.

However, these same individuals owned people as slaves, held extremely narrow views of human sexuality and gender, and believed in the derisible notion of absolute right and wrong. Numerous books and articles have been published explaining the flawed views of our nation's founders, our early leaders, and the disastrous consequences resulting from many of their policies and decisions.

Most in our culture believe that the death of the church in 2061 has brought considerable benefits to our nation. But there have been some other unfortunate casualties in the aftermath of its demise. This change in the foundational beliefs of a people has ushered in the good, the bad, and the ugly.[52] The purpose of this chapter is not to analyze every change in our society since the death of the church. There are a few areas, though, worth highlighting in each of the categories mentioned in the preceding sentence.

THE GOOD

First, most Americans would agree that there is much good result-ing from the death of the church. At the top of the list would be societal freedom from unreasonable restraints on behaviors histor-ically condemned by Christians. This includes numerous archaic ideas on marriage, abortion, sexual choices, gender assignments at birth, and other so-called moral regulations on human behavior.

A case in point is an advertisement campaign featured during the 2023 Super Bowl between the Kansas City Chiefs and the Philadelphia Eagles. The first television ad urged viewers to be more childlike and featured kids of different races embracing each other. A second ad showed images of violent confrontations before displaying text reading: "Jesus loved the people we hate."

New York Congressperson Alexandria Ocasio-Cortez imme-diately went on the attack after these two commercials aired and posted:

> Something tells me Jesus would not spend millions of dollars on Super Bowl ads to make fascism look benign.[53]

Representative Ocasio-Corez's statement was met with a firestorm of criticism from Christians. However, in the years following, the congressperson's assessment of Christians and Christianity became the majority view of Americans. While most Christians appeared benign (as was displayed in these Super Bowl ads), it is now commonly believed that their ideas were and are harmful to our nation. In the opinion of most Americans, *fascism* is an excellent description of these teachings. Many in our nation believe they suffered unnecessarily because of the narrow-minded views of those in the church.

Although unimaginable now, homosexual relationships were illegal during the first two centuries of our country's existence. Sodomy laws punished those in same-sex relationships. For most of the years in which marriage was an institution in our nation, states would not issue marriage licenses to homosexual couples. Polygamists were banned from marrying one another. Businesses, schools, and non-profits regularly dismissed employees for violating so-called "morality clauses" included in their contracts. Engaging in a sexual act with another individual could easily be a fireable offense. For many years, our nation had no laws protecting employees from termination over these violations, even when the violations did not negatively affect their work performance. Teachers, administrators, and college professors were routinely dismissed simply over a physical relationship with a student, even when the relationship didn't interfere with the employee's job duties.

Moreover, there were many cases of our nation becoming needlessly infatuated with the activities of a public figure, causing more important issues to be neglected. Nearly one hundred years ago, the gears of the United States government ceased turning when President Bill Clinton had a sexual relationship with a White House staffer named Monica Lewinsky.[54] When reports of this supposedly scandalous affair surfaced, a major, costly investigation ensued. The Congress of the United States ceased working on matters vital to the health of this country. Instead, they listened to hours of testimony about who was where and doing what with whom in the Oval Office. Eventually, the House of Representatives impeached President Clinton, charging him with lying under oath and obstructing justice. However, the Senate did not vote to convict the president, and the government returned to working on more important matters. Today, it is unimaginable that a public figure would be scrutinized in such a manner over a consensual sexual relationship with a coworker.

The vast majority of American citizens would agree that the tremendous *good* resulting from the demise of the church is the freedom individuals now have to live without restraints. As long as an action does no harm in the way that the person would define harm, then it must be accepted by others in society. To advocate for moral absolutes—as was common through most of our nation's history—felt suffocating to so many in our culture. Since the decline and death of the church, there has been a casting off of what most consider to be prudish, puritanical restrictions on human behavior.

As well, our government agencies have managed to keep the few Christians remaining in our nation from engaging in the public debate with what is viewed as hate speech, dogmatic beliefs, and ridiculously outdated religious absolutes. Arguably, the genesis of this enforcement dates to 2023, when the Federal Bureau of Investigation received criticism from then-Senator Jim Jordan for an "apparent plan to monitor Catholics out of its Richmond, Virginia, office for any suspected domestic terrorism."[55] A memo issued by this office reportedly led to a Catholic priest and a choir director being questioned as potential domestic terrorists because of their religious beliefs. While the memo and resulting actions of these agents were condemned by a few government officials in 2023, this is now a standard, expected duty of the Federal Government. No senator or congressperson today would criticize or condemn any agency for monitoring the religious beliefs of American citizens.

As well, most would agree that the death of the church has enabled our culture to offer more protections for our children. For example, the most vulnerable in our society are those in need of foster care. In September 2023, the Department of Health and Human Services issued new rules regarding the placement of LGBTQ+ children in foster homes. These new guidelines guaranteed that traditional Christian views on sex and marriage would not be allowed for foster parents caring for an LGBTQ+ minor. [56]

In 2029, HHS updated and clarified this policy. LGBTQ+ affirmation language was required in every state's foster care agreement with any parent or parents. No individual was allowed to serve as a foster parent without signing this agreement. Noting that any child has the potential to join the LGBTQ+ community, these belief agreements became standard practice and are still enforced today. Children cannot be subjected to any guardian with non-affirming values.

There are countless other examples of how the death of the church in America has brought an elevated level of freedom to our society. Citizens can live as they choose without condemnation. No one is subjected to the judgmental stares of Christian neighbors, coworkers, teachers, or those in public office. The threat of Bible verses and passages being posted across social media platforms has been eliminated. Offensive "manger scenes" are no longer part of our winter light celebrations. Religious ideas have been removed from public debates regarding any proposed legislation. No one hears a politician evoke god or the Bible in a speech on the House or Senate floors.

Today, most of the population would agree that America is truly a free nation only because we are finally free from the shackles of religion.

THE BAD

However, America in 2071 certainly isn't all rainbows and unicorns. While it is impossible to draw a direct correlation between the death of the church and all the societal ills of our day, it is possible that there have been a few adverse effects resulting from the demise of Christianity. I've chosen three specific problems created from a post-Christian world: a declining economy, a declining population, and a less-charitable culture. All three are interwoven in such a way that they are both causes and effects of one another. I explain this in the following pages.

Until 2029, the United States was the largest economy in the world. However, China's financial boom in the early 2000s moved it from the 13th largest economy in 2000 to the second largest economy just ten years later.[57] For almost twenty years, it remained in second place, finally overtaking the United States in 2029 to become the undisputed world economic power.

Over the next ten years, our nation steadily moved down the list of economies as measured by Gross Domestic Product.

In 2031, for example, when the Chinese *Renminbi* replaced the U.S. Dollar as the world currency, the United States fell from being the third largest economy to fifth, just behind India. Our economy continued to falter and flutter throughout the 2030s. By 2040, the United States had fallen out of the top ten world economies. In recent years, the United States has moved in and out of the top twenty-five.

Economists will point to several causes for the financial downturn. The declining population rate has certainly been a significant factor. One of the reasons our economy lags behind Korea, for example, is that our population is now less than that of this expanding nation. After the reunification of North and South Korea in 2041, the new nation's population exploded. The rise in this nation's birth rate has fueled their ever-expanding economy.

The United States, in contrast, has experienced a marked population decline since the census of 2030. The development of the fetus-dissolving abortion pill *Pregx* in 2038 allowed birthing-persons a low-cost option to effectively end an unwanted pregnancy. Additionally, throughout the 30s and 40s, an increasing number of birthing-persons of child-bearing age chose relational disconnection as their preferred lifestyle. Like most Americans, they found communal fulfillment and entertainment through artificial intelligence and virtual reality generators. Compared with previous generations, teenagers and young adults are far less likely to engage in sexual intercourse. Relational and physical needs were and are frequently satisfied through virtual connections and experiences.

Moreover, as the economic growth of the United States waned, so did immigration. Migrants from Central and South America found greater financial opportunities in Mexico than in the United States. During the first two decades of the twenty-first century, immigrants from other nations served to backfill the declining birth rate among American citizens. Since the 2040s, the flow of legal and illegal immigration has dwindled to less than 15,000 persons annually.

Quite ironically, over the last twenty years there has been a flood of illegal immigration from the United States into Mexico. This nation's growing economy has been a magnet for Americans in search of financial opportunities. Due to the limited legal immigration options, though, many Americans have sought underground networks into Mexico. However, the construction of the *Grande Muro* ("big wall") on the Mexican side of the Rio Grande in 2066 has dramatically reduced unlawful entries into that nation.

While the population decline cannot be blamed fully on the death of the church, Christians did typically promote the idea of a birthing and non-birthing person living together in a committed relationship. Procreation, in most cases, was a normal part of this relationship. As well, churchgoers historically had more children than those who did not attend church. In 2022, for example, devoted churchgoing birthing-persons had an average of 2.1 children in their lifetime, while non-churchgoing birthing-persons had an average of 1.4 children in their lifetime.[58] Naturally, as the number of Christians declined, the overall population did as well.

An additional link between our nation's declining economy and the death of the church can be seen in the loss of productivity among American workers. Christians believe in an unseen, unprovable god who is supposedly all-powerful and all-knowing. While this belief is completely unreasonable, it did lead to some positive outcomes in our culture. One was the notion that they were to work hard for their employer whether this employer was or was not present and watching their performance. Since the eyes of their "god" were always watching them, they believed they had an obligation to be honest and work diligently.

One archived post from the old career-oriented social media platform *JobLink* contained the musings of a restaurant owner in Washington, D.C. The following post was dated August 2029:

> I'm so tired of this entitled generation. I hire some college kid to work as a server, and they immediately tell me the days they can't work and what they will and will not do and how much they expect to be paid. They won't lift a finger beyond what is technically "their job." If they see a piece of trash on the floor, they won't pick it up unless I specifically tell them to clean up the dining room floor.
>
> The exception I've found are Christian college students. I don't care much about god or the Bible, but I do respect the way these Christian kids work. They will clean the tables of other servers or even help clean the kitchen if we aren't busy. They are dependable and treat my restaurant like it's their own. I've overheard one of them talking about working not so much for me but "for the Lord." I've been tempted to say, "Then let the Lord write your paycheck," but I really don't want them to quit!

This type of work ethic described above is now virtually nonexistent in the American labor force. There are still those who work hard, but only if it brings personal gain. The loss of Christians in the workplace has contributed to our nation's economic decline.

Additionally, our nation has become a less charitable society. In 2023, a report by the Better Business Bureau's department on charitable giving described the change in how most Americans viewed their charitable giving:

> ...for the first time since the group started tracking trust for different charity categories (in December 2017), religious organizations (defined as "houses of worship and other religious charities") are not on top.[59]

The report went on to explain that while 32 percent of American adults claimed to have a high trust in religious organizations in 2017, this number dropped to 26 percent in 2022.[60] Over the next several decades, the trust of American citizens in religious organizations continued to erode. By 2055, the percentage of giving to Christian charities was so insignificant that no organization bothered to gather the data. As a result, numerous Christian charities have effectively "gone out of business" in the last three decades. During this same time, the decline in our national economy has led to a greater need for charitable organizations. The austerity measures imposed in 2038 after the national debt crossed $100 trillion led to extensive cuts in government social programs (along with a drastic reduction of our nation's military forces). Non-profit charities simply haven't been able to fill the gap due to the decline in giving. In 2022, for example, Americans gave nearly $500 billion to charities.[61] By 2040, that number had dropped to less than $100 billion. The loss of Christian philanthropies has undoubtedly been a major contributing factor to this decline.

As mentioned earlier, the rejection of Christian parents serving in the foster care system has created a tremendous vacuum in our children's services agencies. For many years, Christians represented the majority of those serving as care-givers in state foster care systems. They claimed this was a part of their calling, "to care for orphans and widows." While many would agree that the removal of non-affirming Christians from these agencies has benefited our children, there is now a massive void in care. Today, our nation has nearly 400,000 children in the foster care program. The latest estimate is that almost 300,000 are housed in group homes. There are not nearly enough families willing or able to serve as caregivers for these children.

These are only a few of the less-than-desirable realities we now face in post-Christian America. But these declines are certainly not the most distributing aspects of our society since the death of the church.

The Ugly

The 1999 science fiction movie *The Matrix* portrays a world in which artificial intelligence has subjugated humans and uses their bodies as energy sources. Physical bodies are trapped in pods while their minds exist in a virtual world, the *Matrix*. The story is about a few individuals escaping from this imaginary world and fighting against these learning machines. One of these rebels, however, decides to betray his fellow comrades. He meets with the computers in the confines of the virtual world. While seated at a restaurant negotiating the terms of their agreement, this human character dines on a steak placed before him and proclaims:

> You know, I know this steak doesn't exist. I know that when I put it in my mouth, the Matrix is telling my brain that it is juicy and delicious. After nine years, you know what I realize? *Ignorance is bliss.*[62]

Although our citizens would agree that the claims of Christianity have been scientifically proven false, there is a sense of hope and purpose that has been lost in our nation since the death of the church. Perhaps, ignorance really is bliss. America's loss of religion has caused a malaise[63] to blanket the population.

This national darkness is a result, in part, of the extreme isolation experienced by most in our culture today. The digital world in which we live has led to loneliness becoming an epidemic. Even seventy years ago, before the advancements we currently have in virtual reality, government officials expressed concerns about this growing phenomenon in our society. A 2023 report by the Surgeon General entitled *"Our Epidemic of Loneliness and Isolation"* highlighted this growing struggle among Americans. One particularly insightful paragraph read:

> Loneliness is far more than just a bad feeling—it harms both individual and societal health. It is associated with a greater risk of cardiovascular disease, dementia, stroke, depression, anxiety, and premature death. The mortality impact of being socially disconnected is similar to that caused by smoking up to 15 cigarettes a day.[64]

This "Loneliness Epidemic" has continued to plague our nation, especially as we have been less and less physically connected as a society. A social media post from 2028 stated the following:

I have 562 followers on Instagram. I follow 1000 other people. I interact with thousands of people every week through my phone, but I have no one to talk to. I'm just so damn alone.

Although this would never be printed today, a May 2023 opinion piece in the *Washington Post* praised the value of religion in our American culture. The author highlighted the positive aspects of faith and participation in houses of worship. This writer, as well, quoted the following from a 2021 paper examining numerous sociological divides in our nation:

Americans who are members of a place of worship are much more likely than those who are not to volunteer in the community at least a few times a year (47 percent vs. 23 percent), talk to someone in their community they do not know well (64 percent vs. 54 percent), and attend a community meeting or local event (60 percent vs. 41 percent)." They are also "more likely than others to feel connected to their neighborhood and the people who live there (58 percent vs. 46 percent).[65]

Simply put, the death of the church has contributed to the creation of a disconnected culture. Today, the majority of

Americans (73 percent) live alone. Houses, condominiums, and apartments have become increasingly smaller in size to adequately meet the needs of our mostly single society. Americans have gravitated toward isolation. Physical interaction with others is no longer a priority.

A 2039 comment on the virtual reality platform *MyWorld* summarized then and now the lifestyle of most Americans:

> I've lived in a 500-unit apartment complex for two years, but I've literally never met a single neighbor. My food is delivered to my door. I work remotely and I socialize virtually. I haven't left my apartment in a month. I probably should go outside, get some fresh air, and meet some people. Maybe I will after I go to this beach party in Aruba. By the way, my avatar is awesome!

I found numerous articles and blogs by Christian pastors and leaders warning against the perils of this technological isolation. An archived blog from 2031 by one Christian pastor bemoaned what he called a "forsaking of the assembly." He noted the heavy bent in our culture toward living in a digital world at the expense of actual relationships. Forty years ago, this pastor offered the following observations:

> No one has a conversation in which they look each other in the eyes. They just text or DM one another. Most people cannot go a day—or even an hour!—without looking at their phones. We wake and check our phones. It's the last thing we do before we go to bed. And we can go all day

without human interaction as long as we have this digital pacifier within our reach.

As a culture, we are headed down an extremely precarious path. The Bible warns us in numerous places about the dangers of isolating oneself. For example, Proverbs tells us that [redacted] and in Ecclesiastes we read [redacted]. I'm thankful that some sociologists and medical professionals are starting to embrace these truths. I just love it when science finally catches up to the Bible!

As the number of Christians in our nation declined, the influence of pastors and other church leaders did as well. Warnings like the one above fell on deaf ears. This disconnectedness as our new normal has led to what many sociologists have dubbed a "national melancholy." We seem to be a people who are isolated, lonely, and hopeless.

Additionally, the freedoms we now enjoy to fulfill our natural desires have left some with hollow emotions and feelings of meaninglessness. Parts of a journal left by a prominent medical surgeon who took his own life in 2033 were later published in a book by his oldest daughter. The book told the story of her father's incredible discoveries and his contributions to the medical field. She also wrote honestly about her father's emotional battles. Although a brilliant surgeon, he struggled with finding happiness in his life. This was especially the case in his romantic relationships. He admitted to numerous affairs during his marriage. After his divorce, he lived with a girl who was half his age. However, he soon discovered that she wasn't "the one." They went their separate ways, he dated other women, then began dating men, thinking perhaps that he was denying his true sexuality. For a season, everything was new and exciting. But eventually, the thrill was gone. He found that he was discontent and restless, trying to find something in life that would fill his soul.

This surgeon's final journal entry read, in part:

One day I woke up and realized that my unhappiness was because I was actually a woman trapped in a man's body. That's why I had been attracted to males. It wasn't enough for me to be a guy and be with other guys. I needed to become who I really was inside. So, I took hormone therapy and I had gender reassignment surgery. And I continued to date and sleep with men. Once again, I found myself feeling empty. Even after my gender transition, I was unfilled. There was still something not quite right in my life. Each time, at the end of the night... or the next morning as I looked over at this person in my bed whose name I struggled to remember... I would think, "Why can't I just find that something that will make me happy?"

Today, I woke up early but stayed in bed until noon, looking back on my life and thinking about my decisions. I've tried everything. I've denied myself no pleasure. I've fulfilled every physical desire.

And yet.

And yet.

Numerous other articles, blogs, and books all referenced the growing dissatisfaction by large segments of our population. For many, throwing off the religious rules and regulations hasn't led to a sense of freedom, but discontentment and depression. These self-indulgent, unrestrained lifestyles have caused many to feel trapped, overwhelmed, and hopeless.

This new reality is most definitely the "ugly" aspect of the post-mortem church. Depression, anxiety, and suicide rates have all skyrocketed. In 2059, the FDA approved the suicide drug *Endall.* After twenty hours of mandatory counseling, a medical doctor is allowed to write this prescription for patients suffering from extreme anxiety or depression. They can then quickly and easily die as they desire, in their home or any other environment of their choosing.

While the dignity of this option is to be praised, the extreme popularity of *Endall* has been a great concern among medical professionals.

A 2064 article written by Dr. Terry Springfield in *Modern Psychology* analyzed this growing crisis in our nation:

Much has been written about the increase in homicide and suicide rates among the American population. Sure, life is life. The worth of a human life is no different from a cow, a dog, a tree, or a cockroach. To say otherwise denies the basic facts of science. We are all simply products of the evolutionary process. Our ancestors were single cell amoebas. Certainly, our biological composure is more complex, but in no way does that give us a claim to greater value. All of life is simply part of this huge cosmic accident called planet Earth. As a scientist, I cannot deny these facts.

Yet, as a psychologist, my concern is that this reality has led not to more respect for non-homosapien life forms, but a devaluation of human life. Rather than becoming vegan and working to protect all of life, our culture has instead shrugged its collective shoulders at the termination of any living entity.

I'm not sure that we have fully uncovered the reasons behind this perspective of most Americans. Even though anti-depressants are now freely available as over-the-counter medications, suicide rates have continued to skyrocket. In 2061, for example, this was the leading cause of death among all age groups under fifty years old. This has become the epidemic of our time. Our President and Congress need to do more to solve this problem before we simply no longer exist as a people.

Sadly, these statistics have only worsened since Dr. Springfield wrote this article several years ago. Our nation has continued to battle, quite unsuccessfully, the plague of depression, anxiety, and suicide. Hopelessness is rampant. Existentialism is the dominant philosophy of the day. A graduate student from The University of the West recently posted the following thoughts on social media:

You're born, you go to school, you work, you have a little sex, you take a few vacations, you retire, and then you die. And that's it. Honestly, what's the point of it all?

To date, the post has been shared by two million users. This sentiment resonated with a large portion of the American population. The ugliest reality of our nation today is that we are a sad, lonely, and hopeless people.

FINAL THOUGHTS

Perhaps it was inevitable. Christianity, in its history, has slowly moved westward. Beginning in the Middle East and Asia Minor, it spread to Greece, Italy, and throughout Europe, eventually reaching the lands that would become North and South America. As Europe came to be the seat of Christendom, the church in the Middle East and Asia died. While the church boomed in America, it died in Europe. Now, it has died in America and moved westward once again. Unquestionably, the heart of Christianity lies in China. India, Pakistan, Indonesia, Malaysia, and Korea all have large Christian populations. Churches in these nations are thriving.

In my research of the church in America, I stumbled upon an old song written by a Christian musical group, *Hillsong*. This group came out of a church that existed for several decades in Australia but, for many of the reasons listed above, ceased to exist in the 2040s. This song, *King of Kings*, was sung by many American churches in their worship services. The lyrics included, in part, the following verse:

> And the Church of Christ was born
> Then the Spirit lit the flame
> Now this gospel truth of old
> Shall not kneel, shall not faint [66]

In America, however, the gospel truth of old did kneel. And fainted. Apparently, the same Church of Christ born in Jerusalem around AD 33 also died in the United States on June 12, 2061.

Today, the church in America remains buried in the ground. Younger Americans are, generally, completely unaware that it once lived and thrived. Some who do know about the church would happily dance on its grave.

But most just do not care.

Acknowledgements

I met Thom Rainer in Houston, Texas, in 2017. That spring, I participated in a pastor's leadership training conference hosted by the Vanderbloemen Search Group, and Thom was the featured presenter in a morning session. Although he was technically a stranger, I felt I already knew Thom. Ten years prior, someone handed me the book he coauthored with Eric Geiger, *The Simple Church*. I read it in two days and highlighted nearly every line on every page. I later asked Thom, "If you highlight everything in a book, have you, in fact, highlighted nothing?"

Two years later, our church had just completed a major building project. I was exhausted and struggling to find vision for my ministry. My assistant at the time did some research on resources for pastors. She came to me and said, "I've found one I think you'll like. It's called *Church Answers*."

"I've never heard of it" I replied.

"Thom Rainer leads it."

"Okay, I have heard of him."

It was almost six years ago when I joined Church Answers. Thom has an unrelenting passion for the local church, and his ministry is focused on equipping those who lead these churches. He has served as a mentor and resource for me as well as thousands of other pastors in the United States and around the world. I owe him a debt of gratitude for his guidance and for his willingness to publish this book.

Additionally, I'd like to thank Chuck Lawless, a professor at Southeastern Seminary in Wake Forest, North Carolina. Chuck served as the content editor for this book, and Chuck has a great eye for detail. I received his first round of feedback and felt like a student in his class who had failed his first exam. Splashed across the pages was copious amounts of proverbial red ink. My first reaction to his comments was, "I'm glad I'm not one of his students." However, upon further reflection, I realized that his critiques would make my book into a better product—just as I'm sure his rigorous expectations of the men and women in his classes make them into better ministers of the gospel. I'm thankful that he was willing to be brutally honest with me about the first draft of this book.

As well, I'd like to thank several of my beta readers: Jeff, Tracy, Phil, Stephen, and Philip. Your feedback was invaluable. And to my wonderful wife, Katie—my best and most faithful beta reader—thank you for all your encouragement.

Finally, I would like to thank the community of faith called Northway Church, a local body of believers in Macon, Georgia. For the last 17 years, I've had the opportunity to pastor this faith family, and it has been one of the greatest joys of my life. In fact, a few early readers of my book suggested that I add a chapter offering some measure of hope; the book ends on such a sour, dismal note, at least for those of us who are followers of Christ.

I didn't want to do that. My goal was to allow reader to feel the shock and see the reality of what will happen if the church in America continues in the same direction. However, if you are after hope, then I invite you to attend a worship service at Northway Church. You will find the antithesis of what you read in this book: a growing community of Christ-followers who love the Lord, love the church, and love the city in which we live.

Every Sunday, when I stand before this congregation, I have tremendous hope that the words you've read in this fictional book will remain exactly that: fiction.

ENDNOTES

PROLOGUE

[1]   https://news.gallup.com/poll/341963/church-membership
-falls-below-majority-first-time.aspx
[2]   https://faithcommunitiestoday.org/wp-content/uploads/
2021/10/Faith-Communities-Today-2020-Summary-Report.pdf
[3]   https://www.thegospelcoalition.org/article/great-dechurching/

INTRODUCTION

[4]   https://www.historynet.com/scotus-101-prayer-public-schools/
[5]   https://www.law.cornell.edu/wex/defense_of_marriage_act
_%28doma%29
[6]   https://www.christianpost.com/news/obama-lied-about-
supporting-traditional-marriage-in-2008-former-advisor-david-
axelrod-reveals-in-new-book.html
[7]   https://www.law.cornell.edu/wex/defense_of_marriage_act
_%28doma%29

Chapter 1

[8] https://www.theologyofwork.org/the-high-calling/daily-reflection/why-worship-wars-never-should-have-happened

[9] https://sowhatfaith.com/2022/12/27/the-only-major-denomination-that-keeps-growing/

Chapter 2

[10] https://www.pewresearch.org/religion/2022/09/13/how-u-s-religious-composition-has-changed-in-recent-decades/

[11] https://www.breitbart.com/faith/2019/10/18/pew-u-s-christian-population-in-freefall-12-drop-in-ten-years/

[12] https://www.graphsaboutreligion.com/p/where-did-the-southern-baptist-convention

[13] https://churchanswers.com/blog/the-death-of-evangelism-seven-unacceptable-responses/

Chapter 4

[14] https://www.huffpost.com/entry/the-gospel-according-to-christopher_b_2231094

[15] https://graceonlinelibrary.org/controversial-issues/liberalism/christianity-and-liberalism-doctrine-by-j-gresham-machen/

[16] https://fbcxmacon.org/travelers-on-a-journey/

Chapter 6

[17] https://www.firstthings.com/article/2022/02/the-three-worlds-of-evangelicalism

[18] https://www.democratandchronicle.com/story/news/2022/11/04/rochester-diocese-pay-55-million-sexual-abuse-claims/69617755007/

[19] https://www.houstonchronicle.com/news/investigations/article/Southern-Baptist-sex-abuse-timeline-17194777.php

[20] https://www.christianitytoday.com/news/2021/february/ravi-zacharias-rzim-investigation-sexual-abuse-sexting-rape.html

[21] https://www.barna.com/the-porn-phenomenon/

[22] https://www.foxnews.com/us/nearly-350-k-12-educators-arrested-child-sex-crimes-2022

[23] https://www.theguardian.com/film/2023/sep/06/boy-scouts-america-documentary-netflix

Chapter 7

[24] https://research.lifeway.com/2021/05/13/are-more-pastors-quitting-today/

[25] https://www.christianitytoday.com/news/2021/september/john-macarthur-covid-settlement-california-church-grace-com.html

[26] https://apnews.com/article/politics-us-supreme-court-california-coronavirus-pandemic-ea77004949becf4b74f9b98930ddec18

[27] https://www.law.cornell.edu/constitution/first_amendment

Chapter 8

28   https://www.foxnews.com/media/petition-seeks-ban-hate-speech-loudoun-county-school-board-meetings

29   Ibid.

30   https://www.aclu.org/news/lgbtq-rights/what-you-need-to-know-about-the-respect-for-marriage-act

31   https://www.cnn.com/2022/11/29/politics/same-sex-marriage-vote-senate/index.html

32   https://www.lifesitenews.com/news/gop-senator-warns-same-sex-marriage-bill-is-democratic-weapon-against-religious-conservatives/

Chapter 9

33   https://www.nbcnews.com/feature/nbc-out/martina-navratilova-apologizes-calling-trans-athletes-cheats-n978971

34   Ibid.

35   In September of 2016, Democratic candidate for President Hillary Clinton referred to the supporters of her opponent, then Republican candidate Donald Trump, as a "basket of deplorables." The term came to signify those with old-fashioned views on cultural issues, chiefly regarding marriage and sexuality.

36   https://www.foxnews.com/us/nyc-judge-polyamorous-relationships-perhaps-time-has-arrived?dicbo=v2-b8677619b20aaffaeb8ae1a75d7a2a93

37   https://www.pbs.org/wgbh/americanexperience/features/mormons-utah/

[38] https://www.psychologytoday.com/us/blog/hide-and-seek/201509/when-homosexuality-stopped-being-mental-disorder

CHAPTER 10

[39] https://churchfiduciary.com/retired-minister-housing-allowance/

CHAPTER 11

[40] https://www.foxnews.com/lifestyle/kirk-cameron-denied-story-hour-slot-public-libraries-faith-kids-book

[41] https://www.newsmax.com/US/christian-bakers-gay-wedding/2013/09/02/id/523439/

[42] https://www.christianpost.com/news/christian-business-gay-marriage-iowa-forced-close-harvest-bible-church.html

[43] https://www.theguardian.com/us-news/2020/apr/19/questions-mount-over-christian-group-behind-central-park-covid-19-hospital

[44] https://www.foxnews.com/media/arizona-school-board-member-district-should-reject-hiring-teachers-with-christian-values-not-safe

[45] This word is reportedly used in the Christian Bible to describe homosexual acts.

Chapter 12

[46] https://www.foxnews.com/media/washington-teacher-says-schools-keep-students-info-secret-christo-fascist-parents

[47] https://www.washingtonpost.com/education/interactive/2023/homeschooling-growth-data-by-district/

[48] Ibid.

[49] https://www.ed.gov/news/press-releases/us-department-education-office-federal-student-aid-fines-grand-canyon-university-377-million-deceiving-thousands-students#:~:text=The U.S. Department of Education,the past four award years.

[50] https://www.cnn.com/2016/11/03/us/penn-state-fine-sandusky-case/index.html

[51] https://www.npr.org/2019/09/05/757909245/michigan-state-university-to-pay-4-5-million-fine-over-larry-nassar-scandal

Conclusion

[52] "The Good, the Bad, and the Ugly" is the title of a 1966 western starring Clint Eastwood as "the Good," Lee Van Cleef as "the Bad," and Eli Wallach as "the Ugly."

[53] https://nypost.com/2023/02/13/aoc-accuses-christian-super-bowl-ad-of-making-fascism-look-benign/

[54] https://www.history.com/this-day-in-history/president-clinton-impeached

[55] https://www.foxnews.com/media/fbis-attack-pro-life-catholics-bidens-america-jim-jordan-warns

56 https://www.acf.hhs.gov/media/press/2023/hhs-announces -historic-child-welfare-package-expand-support-and-equity-child

57 https://www.investopedia.com/insights/worlds-top-economies/

58 https://ifstudies.org/blog/americas-growing-religious-secular-fertility-divide

59 https://give.org/news/article/bbb-s-give.org-study-religious-organizations-are-no-longer-the-most-trusted-charities-among-american-adults

60 Ibid.

61 https://www.nptrust.org/philanthropic-resources/charitable -giving-statistics/

62 Wachowski, Lana, and Lilly Wachowski. 1999. *The Matrix*. Village Roadshow Pictures, Groucho II Film Partnership, Silver Pictures, & Warner Bros.

63 On July 15, 1979, then President Jimmy Carter delivered a nationally televised speech in which they addressed the growing dissatisfaction with life among citizens in this country. Carter's critics dubbed it the "Malaise Speech." Carter never actually used that term.

64 https://www.hhs.gov/sites/default/files/surgeon-general-social-connection-advisory.pdf

65 https://www.washingtonpost.com/opinions/2023/09/10/religion-politics-loneliness-community/

66 Hillsong Worship. (2019). *King of Kings*, On *Awake*. Hillsong Church T/A Hillsong Music Australia.